ACCIDENTAL PURPOSE: AN UNFORESEEN JOURNEY CHANGING LIVES

D. Lynne Cole

This book is dedicated to my parents and to my sons, Brian and Branden. Brian, thank you for being by my side in business and believing in me; you're a wonderful man, and I'm proud of you. Branden, you've found your path in life; never let anyone take you off course in accomplishing your goals, and never forget what you told me: "Wear your seat belt, or I won't"—it saved my life, and I'm proud to be your mother. To Alexandra, you're the daughter I always wanted; you're an amazing young woman, and I'll always be your Mama Bear. And finally, to my wonderful husband, Ray: We've traveled winding roads that led us to each other. You continue to help me cope with the lingering physical pain and give me the courage to overcome my fears and keep moving on.

God's grace is unmerited favor.

CONTENTS

ACKNOWLEDGMENTS

I would like to acknowledge my friends Terrell, Dennis, Roy, Dave, and especially Donna. All of you believed in me, even when I didn't believe in myself. Your kind words of encouragement have meant the world to me, and for that I'll always be grateful.

CHAPTER 1
A MOMENT IN TIME

Afraid and helpless, that's what I felt. His brown eyes were wide, bigger than I'd ever seen. The desperation and panic in them communicated the message that raced through his mind in that split second. I imagine my expression to him somewhat mirrored his image. It was undeniably a look of fear for us both and a final parting of ways, for life as we knew it would never be the same.

Everything happened so quickly. One minute I was a thirty-nine-year-old woman returning in a van from a fun-filled day at a jazz festival with my then-estranged husband, David, and two good friends. The next minute I was unconscious and struggling for my life, after the van had flipped over several times. That day in August 2002 is etched into my memory like a name carved on a tree, remaining as the years pass and the tree grows.

It was a beautiful fall day, with no clouds in sight. David and I had joined our friends, another couple, Steve and Melanie, for the day at the jazz festival. We walked around, absorbing our breathtaking surroundings. We enjoyed the Tuscan feel of the building exteriors, which were draped with winding paths of grapevines. Alongside them, people were laughing and talking at café tables.

As we walked, the four of us laughed and talked as well, indulging in the atmosphere. We drank wine and tasted a variety of foods at booths along pathways that wound through the acreage surrounding the winery. As several dozen children ran around playing and people danced to the jazz band in the music pavilion, I commented, "How great the band sounds, especially the saxophone. The vibration of the music carries through you. They're so loud, I can hardly hear myself think." Yet that reverberating sound felt good; it was like being transported into another world where the sound was all there was. As the acoustics screamed in harmony, the saxophone player seemed to play each note as his emotions dictated.

Then, as we watched several people stomping grapes, I decided I wanted to try. So, holding my wineglass, I stepped onto the platform, took off my white sneakers and socks, and climbed into a large barrel filled with dark-purple grapes. As my foot stepped down, the grapes squished through my toes. My friends laughed at me, and for a moment I wanted everyone to watch me as I pretended to dance like Lucille Ball as she stomped grapes. I lifted my legs and feet while dancing and laughing. Though everyone looked at me like I was crazy, I was having so much fun. When I stepped out of the barrel, David said, "Your feet are blue."

After I put my shoes back on, the bluish-purple color that had stained my feet was visible above my socks. We went on a tour of the winery and saw thousands of bottles of wine being bottled. The tour guide explained all the steps of winemaking, from pressing the grapes in vats to aging and fermenting the wine. The smell of grapes in various stages of fermentation at times overwhelmed me.

At the end of the tour, I noticed an antique-looking metal corkscrew in the shape of a wineglass on top of a bar. I bought it, confident it would perfectly go with my bar at home. I also purchased several cases of assorted wines that I planned to give to friends at a party I was hosting the next weekend. It was a wonderful, fun day, and I didn't want it to end.

During the early evening, as the weather cooled off and the humidity subsided, we headed to Steve's van in the parking lot. A strange feeling came over me, and I didn't want to get into the van. I stood there for a minute, almost as if I needed time to think—which, in retrospect, was pure procrastination. The thought of getting into the van sent an instant, overwhelming nervousness through me. David jumped into the front passenger seat and said, "Come on. Get in." He shut the door while Melanie and I got into the back.

As Steve started the van, I jokingly remarked, "Hey, everyone, put your seat belts on, or my son Branden will be pissed."

It was an odd comment, because I usually never wore my seat beat. Perhaps I thought I'd never need it or that I was invincible. I also hated the way the belt crossed my shoulder and cut into my clavicle. It made me feel as though I were a prisoner being subjected to seat-belt torture. Yet that day I had a strange feeling, like a sudden chill or tingle that swept through me, a gut-wrenching premonition that we all needed to put on our seat belts.

The premonition was especially strange because Branden, my eleven-year-old son, constantly told me to put on my seat belt, or he wouldn't wear his. I never did, but this time was different.

I felt compelled by that strange feeling to buckle up, so I clicked it in. Afterward, I heard the others in the van click theirs. Moments later, Steve pulled out of the parking lot and headed onto the street toward home. There was no oncoming traffic on the road. David asked Steve to turn on some music, and Steve reached for the radio, trying to decide which type of music to listen to. He went through several rock stations before finally selecting some soft jazz. As I sat listening to the music and gazing out the window,

I heard the others talking from what seemed like very far away. My thoughts were on what time my kids would be coming home from staying at their friends' the next day.

As I leaned to my left, positioned to have a clear view between the front bucket seats and with my seat belt pulled tightly against my shoulder, I glanced ahead, looking beyond the car to the road, watching the highway speed by as Steve drove us home. I thought about how much fun we'd had together that day, and I was happy.

A few moments later, however, everything changed. The van began to flip. I wasn't even sure what caused it. Maybe Steve had to swerve to avoid hitting something in the road or to pass a slow-moving car. I wasn't sure at the time, but later I learned he'd had a heart attack and died while driving. His body hit the steering wheel as he lost consciousness, causing him to lose control of the van. In an instant I saw blue, and then green, and then blue and green again. The van kept flipping and turning.

As the van spun over and over, I saw David. Oddly enough, he must have unfastened his seat belt seconds before the vehicle collided with the ditch, the impact of which propelled the van into the air in a violent forward motion. His body was flung around the front seat in midair, causing him to briefly face me, his brown eyes wide open with an emptiness I'd never witnessed before, his face glaring with fear. His head leaned slightly back and then thrust toward me as if he were in slow motion. His body was being tossed around like a doll, along with items that were inside the vehicle with us. At every whip of his neck, his deep-brown eyes were wide and staring at me. Then suddenly he reached his right hand toward me, as if gesturing for me to grab him and hold on to save him from imminent danger. As I subconsciously responded, I reached toward him, trying to grab on out of an instinct to protect him. As my hand brushed across his fingertips, my nails dug into his skin. My thoughts raced as I tried to understand what was happening. Then, with a forceful shriek, the windshield shattered. David was immediately pulled out of the vehicle, as if a vacuum were attached to him. He was gone—sucked out of the van into the void.

As the van continued to flip, I remained safely secured in my seat, firmly supported by the seat belt that I'd been determined to fasten before leaving.

Everything inside the van flew around and hit me, including the cases of wine and the heavy metal corkscrew, which were directly behind my seat. They pounded against the back of my head like huge wooden mallets, each taking its turn shattering glass and spilling liquid against my skull. At the same time, through a blue-and-green haze of sky and grass, I saw that the right-side passenger door had been crushed into my seat, causing glass shards to tear into the skin of my right arm, exposing the muscle, tendons, and bone and causing severe blood loss. From the violent flipping of the vehicle, dirt and mud covered the interior and exterior as the van dug into the grass and dirt until it landed in its final resting place.

The impact of the ground pounding the roof of the vehicle had caused the roof to buckle in half, directly down the middle, and each side had caved in a V shape. The right side of the van had taken most of the impact, causing it to crush down onto my head.

My head was pinned sideways between the roof of the van and my right shoulder, fracturing the vertebrae in my neck in several places. My feet and legs were still in the same position, tucked neatly under the front seat, which was spattered with my blood. My shirt and shorts were soaked in blood as it poured from the wounds on my head and arms.

As I lay there motionless, I was caught in a timeless place where I drifted between consciousness and darkness. For a few moments, I felt the warmth of my blood roll down my face into my eyes, as well as a sense of quiet calm. I heard mumbled words and the beeping of a cell phone. Then, from a distance, came the wailing of a siren. The words and the sounds were like a pounding rock concert, pulverizing my eardrums while blood oozed from my ears. I was trapped and couldn't move, held securely in my seat by my seat belt, which pulled on me like a vise. My head lay placidly on my right shoulder. Soon afterward, the loud whipping sound of helicopter blades overtook my senses; then everything went black.

I saw quick flashes of bright light around me, and then everything became calm and dreamlike. I loved this safe feeling of being deeply at peace; I imagine it was because of the drugs the medics were now giving me.

Oddly, just as this enraptured feeling became a safe place where I knew I wanted to stay, I didn't care about anything. I found myself calmly watching, with no emotion, as the medics cut off my bloodstained shirt while someone to my left slid a syringe into my arm. I felt so peaceful, even though my neck was now trapped in a rigid device. I couldn't understand why my body was covered in blood, my arm unrecognizable.

And why, I wondered, was I now outside and above my motionless body? I was watching their every move; I saw more flashes of light around me, even though I lay motionless with my eyelids closed, but I wasn't scared. Though I had no idea what was actually happening to me, I knew I didn't want to leave this place where nothing hurt anymore.

As I continued to watch myself lying there, covered in my own blood, I felt no pain; in fact, I felt nothing. I saw my two beautiful sons watching television at their dad's house, followed by flashes of my childhood—my brothers and my father as he stood in our kitchen, making pasta. I visualized my son Brian as he rode through our property on our four-wheeler, laughing as Branden and our dog chased him—so many memories flashed by quickly. Colors and bright lights raced through my mind like a reel-to-reel video going from one screen to another.

Within an instant, the pleasant stroll down memory lane was gone, and my godmother, Wilma, was standing before me. She wore a pink dress with small yellow-and-white flowers. Her feet were different from the way I knew them growing up—she hadn't been able to walk without the assistance of a cane or without experiencing severe pain. But now my godmother's feet were perfect, and her hair was no longer gray. Instead it was light brown and was cut short and shaped around her face.

Though Wilma had been dead for more than ten years, she was very much alive as she stood there smiling at me. She appeared to reassure me that everything would be all right.

And I did feel totally at peace and very calm, because I was with my godmother. She looked so beautiful. Finally, smiling placidly, she spoke. "Diana," she said, "don't be afraid. Ben is waiting for you." Her words were calming and reassuring. Ben, who was alive and well, was Wilma's son; I had grown up across the street from them. They were my extended family, and I loved them.

Unable to move, I felt as though I were suspended in a timeless space between the universes, unable to display the emotions that consumed me; all I could do was look at her. Longing for the embrace she gave me during my childhood, I wanted so desperately to reach out and hug her. I always felt safe with her, and the love she displayed for me was powerful. I needed that reassurance, but I was emotionless. Puzzled, I wondered, *Why is she here? And why am I seeing her now?*

But for whatever reason, she was there, and she kept saying to me, "You have nothing to worry about."

Then, suddenly, brief flashes almost blinded me as two people leaned over my shirtless body. One called to me as he methodically opened my jaw and slid a tube down my throat, while the woman on my other side hit my chest with such violent energy that my whole body leaped from the safe spot where it was lying.

Shortly after—I'm not really sure of the time—the beautiful, safe feeling was gone, and in a flash, so was my godmother.

Traffic was backed up for several miles while they airlifted David and I to the closest Level-I trauma hospital. I found out later that a friend of ours was stuck in the traffic as he came back from a meeting and slowly passed the wreckage, having no clue until later that day that his four friends had been in the vehicle.

Meanwhile, my parents and sons arrived at the hospital to find out the bad news. The hospital's pastor had called them; he wasn't permitted to inform them until they arrived of the severity of our injuries or who had survived the accident. Upon my family's arrival, the doctors and pastor told them that I had to be resuscitated while I was being transported in the helicopter to the hospital. All my vital signs were gone, and after several attempts, my heart started beating again. It was indeed a miracle that I was even alive. But my nearly dying once made it more likely that my heart would fail again, and there was an increased chance that resuscitation might not work. My family was also informed about the other passengers. Steve had passed away, and David was in a coma and wasn't expected to survive his head injuries. Steve's wife, Melanie, who had sat beside me in the van, had sustained minor injuries.

My best friend, Donna, arrived with her husband and her brother-in-law shortly after my sixteen-year-old son, Brian, called her to say I had been in a terrible accident. She saw Brian crying, and he looked at her with despair as he told her, "It doesn't look good." Donna then spoke to my mother, who was sitting in a state of shock in the hall outside my room, along with my father. She reached down to console my sons. They knew she was my best friend, and she needed them as much as they needed her. At this point, several other friends and family had arrived and joined my parents and sons in the waiting room to be there when I finally woke up. While my family waited, a doctor came in and told them, "It'll be a few days before we know the outcome of the surgeries to repair her fractured vertebrae. She has a severe head injury and is unconscious."

The doctor then informed my parents of my admission diagnosis: post-motor-vehicle collision, severe closed head injury, periorbital lacerations, right-arm laceration with bone and muscle exposures, C4–C6 cervical spine fractures, Glasgow coma scale rating 3.

They were suspended in time, waiting for some news or guidance regarding what to do.

For several days, family and friends waited and watched for some word on our prognosis. I can imagine how shattering it was for them, not knowing from moment to moment.

CONCLUDING THOUGHT

One moment in time doesn't define who you are or your purpose in life. What defines you is your perseverance to overcome that moment in time.

"Don't be like the people of this world, but let God change the way you think. Then you will know how to do everything that is good and pleasing to him" (Rom. 12:2, CEV).

CHAPTER 2
BEFORE THE ACCIDENT

I grew up in South Florida in a nice neighborhood about fifteen miles from the beach. As a young girl, I was lucky to have several relatives live within walking distance of my home. A cousin lived just around the block and several aunts on the other side of the neighborhood. The family that moved in across the street from me when I was about three years old had three sons. Since they had no little girls, I became the boys' little sister, and this family became my extended family. When I spent the night there, which was often, I shared a bedroom with my godmother, Wilma.

MY EARLY EDUCATION
For a short time, I attended a local elementary school, which was within walking distance from our home. To get there I had to pass a small duck pond and then walk two miles along a canal filled with murky, stagnant water before reaching three schools. The elementary school was the oldest, built around 1940. Just through the front door, the staircase led to the second floor of a large two-story building, which at the time was obviously in desperate need of repair. This school didn't have an elevator or disabled access; back then I'm sure it wasn't mandated.

11

During kindergarten and my first two years of school, I ended up in the guidance counselors' office several times. I wasn't there for disciplinary reasons; rather, my teachers were concerned I had a learning disability. I didn't pay attention during their lectures at times and instead fixed my eyes on objects, usually counting them in my head.

I hated playing on the playground and preferred to sit and stare at the other kids as they ran around, acting stupid. I tried to avoid one kid, John, who wet his pants on a daily basis. I seemed to learn better while staring at the ceiling or some other object, which allowed me to hear others talking without confusing my senses with distractions. I understood every word my kindergarten teacher, Ms. Davis, was saying and at times could quote her lectures verbatim. I hated coloring and scribbling my name in crayon and sitting on the dirty carpet while she wandered around the room, passing gas and snacking on her lunch, all the while telling us to make sure we colored a picture while staying inside the lines. One day I stuck my foot in her path, and down she went, sandwich and all. As soon as she got up, she grabbed my arm and calmly walked me to the principal's office, to which my mother was called.

I argued with Ms. Davis on a daily basis. Her comment to me was always the same: "You're stupid, and you'll never amount to anything." In her defense, she was responding to my daily torments: "You're a boring teacher, and you smell." During one of the many parent-teacher conferences, it was concluded that I was overly analytical and compartmentalized my thoughts, and that was why I never completed my classwork or participated in group projects on her terms. Back then the school system didn't routinely test students to determine whether they had learning disabilities. The guidance counselors took it upon themselves and determined that I needed to be in a private school for children with learning disabilities. At one point I was labeled a kid with autistic tendencies and attention deficit disorder who was highly unlikely to learn at a normal age or grade level.

During one of our meetings, my mother argued with one of the counselors and Ms. Davis, saying that I knew the alphabet at the age of three and had been able to read very well and write in cursive before first grade. The teacher refused to listen and again labeled me as incapable of learning. In our final meeting, my mother refused to place me in a private school for children with special needs. In the guidance counselor's opinion, being placed in that school would allow me to achieve an education, even if it was at a much lower level.

A few weeks later, my parents received a letter from the school board. It read, "After much consideration by the school guidance counselors, it was determined that your daughter has a severe learning disability and is unable to maintain at the same grade level as her peers; therefore she will be removed from public school and assigned tutors for homeschooling."

So homeschooling was set up. I thought this should be fun—I could sleep in and decide which days I wanted my tutors to come to my house. They were scheduled to drop by two days a week for two hours each day. They always came after they finished teaching at their full-time day jobs at the local high school and community college.

I had my whole day to play and have fun—an awesome life for a young kid. My friends were jealous, and they too called me "special" in a derogatory way. Mr. Poplin taught math and science in twelfth grade at the local high school, along with community-college courses, while the other tutor, Mr. Clancy, taught twelfth-grade English. My mother thought, *If Diana has a learning disability, why was she assigned tutors who teach in high-level academic grades?*

When my weekly tutoring sessions began, I was first instructed to select a color of crayon to write with. I always selected red.

During the first year I had home tutors, I noticed that as they lectured, they focused on household pets and basic kindergarten mathematics and made me use my red crayon to spell out simple words as they sounded them out—topics that were taught to young children in prekindergarten.

During each session I found myself staring at a picture on the wall in our dining room while I sat at the table, waiting for the tutor to shut up. I thought that if I had to listen to him blabber any longer, I might scream. To overcome my boredom, while my tutor attempted to teach, I decided to pretend I couldn't understand what he was saying, which increased his frustration. The second year I remember well. I was around nine years old, and I was assigned the same two tutors. Mr. Poplin taught math and science, while Mr. Clancy, who was considered my homeroom teacher, taught English. Before the year started, I was informed that my tutors would focus on more complex lessons, so I assumed this year would be fun. But there was an incident in which Mr. Poplin asked me to complete a simple report on wide-ruled notebook paper in pencil. When he returned the following week for my two hours of tutoring torture, I was excited to hand him my report, which I had completed with such precision and detail. As soon as he glanced at it, he became slightly angry, saying, "I only asked for a simple report, and I get this. Can't you listen?" I had turned in a report on architectural graph paper with depth and detail, and he was accusing me of having one or both of my much-older twin brothers complete it.

How dare he? I thought. So, after he left, I decided I would redo the same report as requested, only this time it would be in red crayon on a torn piece of notebook paper. I was determined to write the paper so it would look like a three-year-old who was just learning how to write had completed it. When Mr. Poplin returned the next day, I thought, *He's an idiot,* as I handed it to him. He actually smiled because I had listened to his instructions.

Finally, midway through the third year and the endless months of pretending to pay attention to both of my tutors, the final straw occurred when Mr. Clancy, exhausted with having me as his student for yet another year, told me, "I deal with thirty high-school seniors at a time in one class, and you, an eleven-year-old girl, are harder to handle than all of them combined." He gave me an assignment, knowing that if I didn't complete it, he could return to the school board and ask to be removed as my tutor. He assigned me to select any book, assured that I would select a children's storybook, and write a one-page book report. *Great,* I thought, *finally something challenging.* My mother and I went to the store, I found a novel that was on the best-seller list, and she bought it for me. Back then there were no online resources.

As soon as I got home, I began reading. I read the entire book in three days and completed a book report, handwritten with pen in cursive. It gave an overview of each chapter and depicted the depth and breadth of the book. When Mr. Clancy arrived, I was so excited that he had actually allowed me to do something fun that I ran up to him as he came through the door, looking exhausted from his full day of teaching and probably regretting he had to show up at my house. I shoved my book report into his hand. This was the first time I'd actually looked forward to his arrival. He glanced at my lengthy handwritten report, neatly written in cursive, with each chapter heading properly centered at the top in the middle of the page. He looked at me with either amazement or exacerbation; I'm not sure. He immediately walked over to where my mother sat and told her I had cheated again. She responded, "She read the entire book and completed the book report herself."

He said, "Then Mr. Poplin and I need to test her out of each grade to measure an accurate academic level."

He finished talking with my mother and left. The following week, I was scheduled for four straight days of intensive testing. The first exam was at fifth-grade level, and then sixth, and then seventh, and then eighth, all the way through to the twelfth grade. *Wow, this was easy*, I thought. We were done; the testing results were complete, and the report was sent to the school board. A short while later, my parents received a letter in the mail stating that I was no longer labeled as having a learning disability; rather, I was highly intelligent and should undergo additional testing. My tutors came to the house for a few more months; we shook hands and said our good-byes.

MY OLDER TWIN BROTHERS

I grew up with twin brothers who were mirror images of one other. Each wore the same clothes without knowing the other had chosen the exact shirt on the same day. Their idea of fun was to confuse other people about who was who.

My brothers were a team, and I, as the little sister, had to endure their brotherly torture. One day I was awakened at five in the morning with one of my brothers on each side of my mattress, holding it and shaking it in the dark, as if I were in an exorcism movie. They had covered their faces with something, so all I could see were shadows from my night-light.

After completing their prank, my brothers got dressed, ran to the bus stop, and went to school. I was still shaken up from being jarred from a sound sleep, so I took a walk to my cousin Gene's house and told him what happened. He laughed and responded, "What are you going to do?" I had no clue how I was going to get even with two older brothers who only wanted to torment me.

As I walked home that afternoon, I passed the small duck pond that led to the elementary, middle, and high schools. The pond didn't have a fountain to circulate the water, and in Florida's summer heat, a stagnant film of dark-green algae thickly skimmed the top of the pond. Since retirees often fed the ducks, the birds stayed close to the pond. They were large, with white feathers, and many of them swam and played in the small pond. As I stood there for a moment in deep thought, still angry with my brothers, I watched the ducks, which had green slime coating their white bodies up to their long, white necks. I then ran as fast as I could to my house to retrieve every cracker and loaf of bread I could find. Next I ran across the street to my godmother's home to get all her bread. She greeted me with curiosity, wondering what I was up to. I headed back to the pond. By this time my intention was to lock the ducks in our backyard behind our large privacy fence while my brothers were at school, knowing they would have to enter the yard when they returned and cross a small path that would be covered in slime-coated ducks.

So off I went to the pond with my brilliant idea reeling through my young mind. When I arrived, there must have been thirty ducks slowly swimming around as if they were taking a nice, warm bath, since the water in this small pond had to be more than eighty degrees. As they swam, their feathers collected the floating slime, duck excrement, and anything else that happened to be floating in the pond that day. *Wow,* I thought, *the more the better.* I knew I didn't have enough bread to entice them to follow me the one block home, so I counted the slices of bread in each loaf, divided by the number of houses I had to pass with the ducks in tow, and started dropping crumbs, at first a larger amount to get them to follow behind me—and they did, all of them. As we passed each home, I tore up the exact number of slices of bread I had calculated. Then I threw it in small pieces to spread around so the ducks would have to race in front of each other to retrieve them, which meant getting a few feet closer to my home.

We were almost there. I continued to feed them one slice at a time as I passed each house, and my plan was working. They were dirty and following me home. We were now on my street, and my house was in sight. Just four more houses to go, and I still had more than a loaf to spare. Our next-door neighbor, Steve, pulled up next to me and stared with a puzzled look, likely wondering, as he usually did, what that girl was up to today. I'm sure he was afraid to ask, so he just stared. Then my godmother's son, Chuck, who was a few years older than me, saw me and ran over. He had stayed home from school that day because of his severe allergies. It was fun when he stayed home, because I always went over to his house and played.

"What are you doing?" Chuck asked. I told him about my plan, and he laughed. He watched as I continued to tear up small pieces of bread as I finally crossed Steve's yard and then my yard. I opened our gate, and all the ducks from the pond followed me inside. I was excited that I was going to get even with my brothers; my plan was working.

I shut the gate and headed toward the house. As I reached for our back door, I noticed the adjacent bedroom door had been left open. It was obvious that my brothers had left their room in a hurry. Clothes were strewn all over the bedroom floor, as usual. I pushed the door open farther and ran inside, knowing that if I got caught now, I'd be in trouble. The ducks naturally followed me into my brothers' bedroom because I was holding the last remaining pieces of bread. By this time they were in a feeding frenzy, almost chasing after me as they vied for another morsel. I went to the dresser and opened every drawer before placing crumbs on top of the dresser. I even laid down my brothers' cologne bottle and placed a slice of bread on top, knowing the ducks would find it. I ran over to both beds, pulled the covers back, and then dropped bread crumbs on top of every pillow and around the sheets. Looking around, I noticed their stereo and beanbag chair. At the time my mind was racing, knowing that if they caught me, it would be a fight with both of them against just me. I tore the bread into small pieces and lightly sprinkled them on top of their record albums and stereo.

I was on a roll. I went to the closet and grabbed clothes that were on hangers, dropping many on the floor. I thought, *Great, now the ducks can have lunch, and then crap and take a nap all in the same spot!* By this time, the algae- and germ-infested ducks, covered in green slime and their own waste, were running rampant inside my brothers' bedroom. They were looking for bread, and when ducks eat, the next natural thing to do is crap. Well, they did a lot of that; my brothers' Doors album was covered in bird droppings.

It was mid-July in Florida, and we lived a few miles from the beach. Back then we didn't have central heating or air-conditioning, so naturally it became very hot and humid in our home during the day, especially in my brothers' bedroom, since it was only marginally insulated.

I was finally finished. *Wow*, I thought, certain I would get into trouble. I closed the door and went across the street as protection, knowing my godmother would give me a great alibi. She loved me, and in her eyes, I could do nothing wrong. She was my savior while I was growing up.

Several hours later, my brothers arrived home from school. As they walked down the street from the bus stop, I stood inside my godmother's home, staring out the window. After they came through the door, I heard them screaming my name. The ducks had been in their room, sleeping on top of everything; white feathers, green slime, and poop were everywhere. The stench was overwhelming by this time, I'm sure; the room would have smelled like a septic tank. I knew they were looking for me. One of my brothers walked halfway across the street and saw me peering through the window at him. I wasn't worried, because I was hiding at my godmother's house, where no one could hurt me.

When my mother returned home from shopping, she heard my brothers screaming and of course blaming me for the mess in their bedroom. As I stared out the window from across the street, I saw ducks being shooed from our house, frantically running in every direction to escape the two erratic young men chasing them. My mother ran to the phone and called my godmother's house, I'm sure to discipline me. When Wilma answered the phone, I heard my mother talking loudly, telling her I needed to get home now. She was determined to reprimand me. My godmother immediately replied, "Diana and I are busy in the kitchen, baking brownies. She's been here with me all day." When I returned later that evening, the mess was cleaned up. I ran into my bedroom and locked the door, and I never got in trouble. I denied everything, saying I saw my brothers leave their bedroom door open, as they sometimes did, and the ducks must have found their way in. No one asked how the ducks got into the closed, fenced-in yard and through the back door, and I wasn't about to offer an answer, but my brothers knew the truth.

After that incident they were actually nice to me. But then one day, while I was playing in the yard, my brother Mark found a nest of cockroaches underneath a rotted pile of wood in the yard. He reached down and grabbed a handful of the large bugs. As his hand touched the nest, several cockroaches crawled up his arm. He walked calmly toward me as they scurried around on his hand and arm, with some falling off along the way. He came up behind me as I sat on the sidewalk, talking with my friend Gina. She noticed him coming toward me with roaches on his arm and got up to run. As soon as I noticed what was happening, I turned around, and suddenly his hand was over my head. As he shook his hand to release the large, crawling cockroaches, several landed in my hair, while others crawled down my tank top. I jumped up, screamed, and ran around. They were everywhere—in my shirt, in my hair, and crawling on my scalp under my barrette. Back then I had long hair that fell several inches below my waist, which made it harder to get them out, since they were tangled within my long braid. My mother heard my screams and came running out of the house. It took several minutes for me to get all the bugs off, and by that time I was overwhelmed and completely grossed out.

I ran through the back door of our home, which led into laundry room. As I stood in front of the washing machine, looking around and still feeling disgusted, I noticed a box of Rit dye, which my mother had used several days before in the washer to dye my jeans back to blue. I was still shaken up from the bugs crawling all over me. I reached for the dye, at first not knowing what I was going to do with it. I slid the box into my pants pocket and walked into my bedroom, which was next to the bathroom. After I entered the bathroom, I turned on the sink to have the sound of water running, thinking I needed a cover-up for being in the bathroom for so long. I leaned into the shower, grabbed the bottle of shampoo that I knew my brothers liked, and emptied the Rit dye package into their shampoo bottle. I shook the bottle so the powder and shampoo would mix and be undetectable. To my surprise, they blended perfectly, except the color changed to a very pretty light blue.

The next morning, when they both got ready for school, my brother Michael noticed the shampoo was blue and commented on it. I said, "Mom just bought that. It comes in a new color." He jumped into the shower, which fogged the mirror from the hot water. The other twin, Mark, quickly followed. As usual, they had to rush so as not to be late for the bus, so neither paid attention upon exiting the bathroom. As soon as Michael went into their shared bedroom, he briefly glanced into the mirror to brush his hair and noticed that his hair was a light shade of blue. As he screamed my name, my second brother looked in the mirror and went insane, shouting as well. Of course, I was in hiding; I knew it would be a two-against-one fight, and I'd lose. They were sent to school that day with their blue hair—the same color as a Smurf—and my instinct to fight back was realized.

THE SMELL OF MOTHBALLS

When I was young, we had an older woman, my mother's aunt Ellie, staying at our home for several months. She perpetually smelled of mothballs—that same overpowering smell that burns your eyes when you walk into a damp, musty closet. As a young girl, I always assumed she was decomposing, and the mothballs were used to cover the smell, which exuded from her pores. I had to share a bedroom with her, smell her, and hear her snore and fart in her sleep. One day she and my mother left to go shopping, and I was home all alone. I'd already been through several weeks of snoring torture with little to no sleep. As I sat in my room, playing, I stared at her bed.

I abruptly stood up, looked at her disgusting, urine-stained sheets, and decided she had to go. I grabbed her mattress and stood it on one side, dragged it along the floor, and shoved it through the doorway and down the hallway, past two bedrooms and a bathroom, tugging and pulling on it as the sheets that smelled of urine from her weak bladder dragged behind. Finally, when I turned the corner into the living area, mattress in tow and the front door in sight, it toppled over onto the floor. I had to crawl underneath it and position myself directly in the middle. The smell was overpowering as my head was shoved into the mattress urine stain. After ten to fifteen minutes of wrestling it into a standing position, I was back on my journey, and out the front door the mattress went, right into our front yard and onto the grass. As I briefly stood next to the mattress, I glanced across the street and noticed my godmother, Wilma, looking out her front window at me. I smiled at her as I headed toward the front door, stomping back to my bedroom, huffing and puffing and mumbling, "She's got to go." Then I slammed my bedroom door and locked it.

My mother arrived home from work shortly afterward to find the mattress in the middle of the yard, where all the neighbors in our middle-class neighborhood with perfectly manicured lawns could see it. She laughed hysterically; to this day she wonders how a skinny twelve-year-old could have dragged a queen-size mattress into the yard by herself.

My godparents were active in their church. On Sundays I was always in tow during church functions and services. I usually stayed at their home on Saturday nights, waking up to the smell of breakfast and knowing that church would follow. My memories of my childhood are mixed. I was raised by a very strong mother who was business-savvy. She too was in a car accident when I was six or seven, and she was placed in a hospital bed that rotated around while her fractured spine healed. She complained that she wanted something to do and decided to study for her contractor's exam while in the hospital. After several months of reading books and studying, she was released from the hospital and took the state boards. She became one of the first women in our state to acquire a building contractor's license.

My mother went on to manage several businesses while multitasking each one to perfection. She once told me that her mind never stopped. She could calculate any complex math problem in her head without using paper or a calculator. I'm certain that when I was a child, she saw the same characteristics in me and thought we were both headstrong. Even as a young child, I wouldn't let anything or anyone get in my way.

Before the accident, at night I would come home from work, cook dinner, clean the house, and spend time with my sons. Many nights, as soon as they went to bed, I stayed up late, sometimes until two in the morning, writing in my journal, and woke up just in time to rouse my children at seven to get them off to school. This routine lasted for months until complete exhaustion took over, and I became sick. And then I started the routine all over again.

My children never knew what I sacrificed as a mother. The stack of overdue bills always seemed incomprehensible. Yes, I wallowed in self-pity for a while, until one day I'd had enough. That was when the little girl who was told by the school counselor that she was overanalytical and had a learning disability took over, and since then I've never looked back.

CONCLUDING THOUGHT

It doesn't matter where you come from or how you were raised. What matters is your determination to change what seems to be an impossible circumstance, whether it it's one event or a childhood riddled with anguish and abuse. Remember, there's someone somewhere to reach out to and ask for help. Take that painful event or circumstance and learn from it; use it to build your character and become someone you can be proud of.

CHAPTER 3

FIGHTING FOR SURVIVAL

I'd been placed in a medically induced coma to allow my brain to heal from my open and closed head injuries. I'd lost an excessive amount of blood, and the doctors weren't sure whether I would live or die. If I lived, they feared I might be paralyzed because of the severity of my vertebral fractures.

The timeline was hazy—what seemed like months of being sedated might only have been days. When the doctors finally decided to bring me out of the coma, I opened my eyes, trying to blink away the film that covered my pupils. Everything seemed so blurred. I could only make out obscure objects; nothing in my view was identifiable. At first I thought I was dead; the atmosphere was both calm and surreal. I noticed a figure standing next to me on the left side of the bed. She had long, brown hair that lay across her chest. At this point I had no comprehension of what had previously taken place or why I was there; I just knew that my godmother's son, Ben, was standing next to me—just as Wilma had said he would be—along with his wife, Mary.

Within a short time, my eyelids became heavy again, and I dozed back off into unconsciousness, only to be woken by what sounded like my youngest son, Branden, saying, "Mom, wake up." I couldn't respond, so I lay there as he continued to call out, "Mom, wake up." I felt a sense of disconnection from reality; I heard him call my name but was unable to respond to his soothing voice.

I wanted to reach toward him, but the numbness in my upper extremities was overpowering. Why couldn't I touch my son? When I was able to finally open my eyes, again all I could see were fuzzy images. At one point the room started to spin. All I could do was blink; I couldn't move or sit up, since a rigid collar was supporting my neck. As my ability to focus on objects improved, I noticed my parents, my son Brian, and my best friend, Donna, staring blankly at me. No one was speaking; they were just staring. I felt like a car on an auction block, with everyone standing around looking at it, watching and waiting to see if someone would buy it.

My eyes darted around the room, since my eyes were the only body parts I could move, and I saw Branden leaning next to my hospital bed. He too was staring at me intently. As I glanced around the room, bouncing from one object to another, the motion made everything in the room spin again. I tried to force myself to blink away the spinning; I felt as if my eyeballs were going to burst out of their sockets.

I noticed the white, sterile walls and the television monitor that was directly in front of me, and suddenly I felt something protruding from my chest. I didn't know what it was; I just knew it felt odd to have something attached to my chest, with cords strewn under the covers like tiny androids, holding me hostage. What was this strange contraption attached to me?

Then someone touched my left forearm, hard enough that I felt the pressure of his or her hand as it pressed against my skin.

I'm not sure who it was, but my mother was leaning in close to me, so close that it almost felt as if she were looking into my thoughts— or maybe she was checking to see if I was breathing. She was glaring at me, and I felt her breath on my skin. At first it looked like she was angry, but it was just that her soft, hazel eyes were magnified behind her glasses.

"Where am I?" was all I could muster from my thoughts, though I don't think my voice was loud enough to be heard. "Where am I?" I mumbled again, barely able to speak through the heavy sedation that was slowly fading from my body. "What happened?" I asked, continuing to blink away the sleepiness.

It felt as if someone were sitting on my chest, and my ribs were crushing in and suffocating me—but why? I had no idea what had taken place or why I was lying in this bed, unable to move.

Then I glanced at my right arm and noticed it was completely wrapped from my wrist to my armpit in white, sterile bandages dotted with spots of blood that had seeped through from the surgery to reconstruct my arm where it had been torn from the muscle and bone. Suddenly I looked at my mother and blurted out, "I saw Wilma!" All I got from her in return was an empty, confused stare; she didn't respond—or if she did, I don't remember. Then my thoughts raced: *Why are they staring at me? Why can't I move?* I started crying. "I saw Wilma," I repeated.

"You were in an accident," my mother said. "You're in the hospital."

Meanwhile, my father just stood there, watching everything, not saying a word. He never really showed emotion, and this time was no different.

My son Brian said, "Mom, you have to rest."

Accident? Hospital? The words echoed through my mind as I tried to think back and piece my memories together. But everything was so vague. I had no memory of the accident; I just remembered seeing my godmother, Wilma.

It took everything I had to stay awake—not that I was alert; I just knew I needed to be near my family. Having them nearby made me feel safe. After some time I couldn't muster enough energy to keep my eyes open, and I surrendered to what I assumed would be a peaceful rest. As quickly as my eyes shut, however, my mind raced with vivid images: the image of the four of us talking and laughing as the highway sped by, and then the green fields and orange groves in perfect rows in the well-maintained orchards that covered the hundreds of acres surrounding the winery.

I remembered every detail of every moment up until the mental screen went blank, and then I didn't remember any more. My thoughts kept reeling back the movie screen in my mind, like an old black-and-white movie playing with no sound. *Where are my friends? Where am I?* Over and over this played until the movie screen in my head went blank.

I must have started crying out loud in my sleep, because a nurse came in and shook me awake. Startled from my dreams, I grabbed for her just as I had grabbed for my husband, David, in those last moments in an effort to save him just before he was hurled through the windshield. But this time was different; I grabbed hold of her lab coat.

When I tried to turn my head to look around but couldn't, I realized my legs were heavy and had no feeling, like when you sleep on your arm and it feels like it weighs more than a hundred pounds as you shake it violently to circulate the blood flow.

The nurse moved away, and my mother stepped up to the bed. Standing next to me, she said, "The doctors said you broke your neck and have a severe head injury, so you're unable to move."

As she talked and repeatedly tried to explain to me what had occurred, I tried to understand the seriousness of my situation. Usually I was full of energy, always the responsible one, taking care of everything in my uniform business, which had been open for a few years, as well as caring for a home and my two sons. But now I wasn't in a position to do anything. I felt a throbbing that started in my head and progressively gravitated into my neck and down my spine to my waist, though I didn't know why it stopped there. This vicious cycle continued again and again, like a jackhammer going up and down on a street, pausing before the throbbing started again.

Soon the pain in my head came faster and stronger with each breath, as if it were coming from my heartbeat, each beat pounding louder and louder. I tried to keep myself from screaming; instead I tried to breathe out the pain or imagine it going away, especially since I didn't want my sons to know my brain felt as if it would explode right out of my skull all over the floor. They were hurting enough inside, seeing their mother lying helplessly in the hospital. As the nurse continued to give me more pain medication, the throbbing seemed to subside for a while, and I'd briefly fall asleep, only to see the vivid scenes from the accident play through my mind before the throbbing started again, and I'd awaken.

I'd never experienced this kind of intense pain before, not even in childbirth, when I was able to handle the pain and deliver two healthy sons naturally. Each episode was more traumatic than the last, and sometimes the throbbing was so intense that I briefly wished I had died in the accident just to stop the pain.

After several cycles of this, exhausted, I finally closed my eyes once more. I was relieved to have some respite from the throbbing pain when a neurologist and a neurosurgeon, along with several other hospital staff members, entered my room and startled me from my five minutes of sleep. Two of them stood at the foot of the bed, asking me, "Do you feel this?" and again, "Do you feel this?"

I mouthed, "No."

One doctor walked up next to my bed and bent down so his face was close to mine. "I need you to wiggle your toes," he said.

I had no clue what they were doing or what he was asking of me; I just stared back blankly. They were poking at my feet and legs for some nerve response. But I just lay there, feeling nothing, and responded, "OK."

After they stopped poking and prodding, one of the doctors leaned in toward me and said loudly, "We're taking you back into surgery," perhaps assuming I was deaf and couldn't hear him. I could hear what he was saying; I just had no idea of the meaning. Suddenly two men came in and wheeled my hospital bed into a larger room that was very cold. My shivering was uncontrollable.

Is this what a morgue feels like? I wondered.

I was now lying facedown on a cold, hard table with my head positioned snugly on top of a padded cushion, like a doughnut that someone sits on to relieve hemorrhoids. Was I on a massage table waiting for a nice, relaxing rubdown? My arms were heavy from the imaginary weight that pulled them toward the floor.

My head was secured in a device, and then I heard a jumble of words and felt a rag or something liquid that was very cold being dragged across the back of my neck. I must have dozed off, because the next memory is fuzzy.

I couldn't understand what the doctors were doing or saying; it was like they were speaking above me as if I were some meaningless object with no name or face. Finally, I felt nothing as this heaviness left me, and I fell into a deep, calm sleep. Later, I found out that the hospital telephoned my mother to tell my family the grim prognosis. "Diana is paralyzed and has no feeling or sensation in her legs," a doctor told her. "We're taking her in for surgery again."

I had a spinal contusion, which meant there was bruising on my spinal column, so they needed to operate again to stabilize three of my cervical vertebrae. "We'll contact you when we know more," she was told. I was sleeping when she and my father left the hospital to go home and get some clean clothes. After receiving the call, they turned the car around, devastated that I was being rushed into surgery again and now aware of the possibility that I might be paralyzed. When they finally reached the hospital, they went directly to the OR waiting area and waited for the doctors.

After the surgery, the doctors spoke with my family and explained that the wire mesh that previously had been inserted into my neck to support my spinal injury had to be removed and replaced with several titanium rods. It might take weeks to know the prognosis. I was wheeled into recovery, where I stayed until I became conscious.

An Episcopalian pastor named Paul came into my room. He had been on call when the accident happened, and he said he had come by that day and sat with me, although I didn't remember him being there. I asked him, "Why did this happen? What did I do wrong?"

"You did nothing wrong," he replied, "and I believe God has a purpose for you, since you survived."

I was so confused. Through my tears, I told him, "I saw my godmother."

He didn't look at me funny like everyone else I had told about this experience. He just listened. Then he reassured me in a calm voice, "It just wasn't your time."

He held my hand and prayed with me. He also left his card, which I kept. Later, on the one-year anniversary of the accident, which happened to fall on a Sunday, my sons and I drove to his church to thank him. As I walked into the huge church, filled with what seemed like hundreds of people, he stood there greeting the members. He glanced in my direction and immediately remembered me from our meeting in the hospital. He thanked me for coming to see him, and I thanked him for being there when I had needed spiritual guidance. We both felt a sense of closure, which I believe everyone needs.

MAKING A LIFE-OR-DEATH DECISION

A few days after my second surgery, the anesthesia was finally wearing off. I awoke to see several people standing near my hospital bed. At first I had no idea who they were, because I was still heavily sedated from the anesthesia and the heavy narcotics that relieved me from the constant pain. I realized that many of the visitors were from my estranged husband's family, since we were still legally married.

Since the number of people who could be in my hospital room at any one time was limited, David's family members came into my room one or two at a time with the same message: "Please. Just sign the form." I didn't understand what they were saying to me; my head was spinning from the narcotics and anesthesia that had obscured even my limited memory of the incidents that had led up to the accident.

"Why are you asking me to sign this piece of paper?" That was all I could muster. Could they even hear me talking? I stared at them, almost certain the questions I still needed answered were jumbled in the thoughts my mind was trying to transfer into words, but I was certain no one could hear me anyway.

At this point I still hadn't been told the details of what had happened or who hadn't survived, because I was suffering from posttraumatic stress disorder (PTSD) and memory loss, so I really didn't know what they wanted. Finally, I realized they wanted me to choose life or death for my estranged, comatose husband, whom the doctors said would most likely never wake up.

I had no idea of the consequences of signing one piece of paper. My last memory of David was when he was staring at me so intently, reaching for me to save him as he flew backward into the void of the windshield.

Where did he go? I thought.

I couldn't grasp the magnitude of the accident and was confused by the question I was being asked. We'd never spoken of our personal wishes in the event that one of us wasn't expected to survive an accident.

After several days of constant visits, my mother realized I shouldn't be left alone, so one day while she was in the room with me, David's sister Lisa walked in and handed me a pen and a piece of paper. I later learned this was a form authorizing the doctors to remove the life support that was keeping her brother alive. "He wouldn't want to live as a vegetable," she said.

Finally, my mother intervened, telling her, "Get out! She doesn't understand what you're asking of her."

His sister withdrew the form and retreated, saying as she left, "I love my brother; I want what's best for him."

Shortly afterward, David's mother barged into the room and boldly waddled past my mother. Towering over me, she said loudly enough that others in the hallway could hear, "I don't agree with what they're asking of you. I think you should give him a chance. Don't sign the form." She added, "Give him a chance. It's God's decision, not yours." My mother threw her out as well.

Just as the room became quiet again, a doctor entered, accompanied by several nurses and several of David's family members marching directly behind them. This time everyone was surrounding my hospital bed like a small army, staring at me.

"Are you willing to end David's life support?" a doctor asked me.

My mother told everyone, "She doesn't understand what happened; go get a judge to order it."

David's father responded, "We tried; he said no." Therefore, any life-or-death decision was up to me once I opened my eyes and became lucid. His family assumed I was mentally competent, even though my mother kept telling them I had no memory or comprehension of the accident.

Not one person, not even the doctor, would listen to her. When I didn't reply, the doctor asked me again, "Will you sign this document so we can end life support?"

"Please sign it," someone from behind the doctor begged.

The doctor told me, "Your husband is in a coma and will be in a vegetative state for the rest of his life. There's nothing more to be done."

Their words echoed in my head over and over, but I couldn't speak. What were they talking about? Why were they looking at me? All I wanted to do was close my eyes and sleep. Finally, I weakly held up my bandaged right arm, with my swollen fingers and blood-splattered bandages, and said, "I can't write."

And that was true; I couldn't write with my right hand, because I was left-handed. But I held up my right arm—maybe it was to show everyone in the room my arm was injured. It was an automatic response at the time, and I'm not sure why I did it. Now, looking back, I'm sure that a power much bigger than me was lifting my injured arm, or maybe subconsciously it was because I didn't want to sign the paper to end David's life.

Only my mother knew I was left-handed and could have easily scribbled an X on that form to end his life. Afterward, she looked at me and asked why I had raised my injured right arm. I replied, "Because it hurts."

For many years I went and visited David in rehab, against his family's wishes. They made it very clear that I wasn't wanted and that he wouldn't have wanted to live like this. It tormented me for years that I was being blamed for his living in a vegetative state.

I've carried a heavy burden of survivor's guilt, knowing that I lived and my life was moving on, and David was suffering in a diminished mental capacity due to the frontal lobe of his brain having been severely damaged when he was thrown through the windshield and also when he landed on the roadway. I continued to struggle with this feeling for twelve years, while he remained in a vegetative state in a nursing home until his passing.

During my time in rehabilitation, I was unable to eat or keep food down, and my weight plummeted to eighty-seven pounds.

The nutritionists tried everything to help me gain my weight back. The pain was so intense that I vomited everything I had eaten every day, which meant I was unable to hold down the cocktail of medications the doctors prescribed, and many days I was too weak to go to physical therapy.

My normal weight was around 115 pounds, and the drastic weight loss caused my eye sockets to become hollow, my cheeks to sink in, and my rib cage and clavicle to protrude. The only form of nutrition I could tolerate was Boost chocolate nutritional shakes, which became my only source of daily nutrition.

One evening I met the nicest nurse who worked third shift. She came in to check on me around midnight when the place was quiet because the rest of the nursing staff had gone home and the other patients were asleep. I was crying, and she asked, "Are you OK?"

I replied, "My head hurts."

Then, briefly, my cries went into hysterics. I tried to explain what I could of what I remembered. "I have little memory of what had happened," I told her. "I have vivid images of my husband's face as he stared back at me, his brown eyes wide open as he disappeared through the windshield." And then I tried to explain what I was feeling and said that every time I tried to sleep, either the pain or the images of the accident would wake me up. I usually woke up soaked in sweat, screaming from my nightly reruns of the accident; it was loud enough to wake up several of the patients on the same floor as me.

REHABILITATION BEGINS

The day I left the hospital, I was placed in a wheelchair and driven to the rehab hospital where I would start my long journey of physical therapy. After arriving on the on the third floor and getting settled into room 308, in the bed next to the door, I looked around at the bleak surroundings, my eyes darting from one object to another. The intake nurse came to see me and explained my therapy schedule. I just sat in the bed, staring past her as she talked, looking over her shoulder as if she were invisible and then glancing down the hall as visitors exited the elevator. At that moment I had no place to go or means to take me there, so all I could do was stare—at the walls, the ceiling, and the other patients' visitors.

My first days in rehab were surreal; my thoughts went back to the accident and always ended on seeing my godmother's face one last time. My first real shower after the accident was challenging, since the hospital was only able to lightly wash my scalp because of the large U-shaped stitches that covered it. Three nursing assistants helped me gently wash and comb the glass and dried blood out of my hair, trying not to touch the scar and surrounding area. I also needed their help to stand and to pivot my body in the walk-in shower. It was overwhelming to ask someone I didn't know to help me get undressed and take a shower. Like most people, I need my independence and need to know I can take care of my basic needs.

I depended on them that day for the basics of care and understood that their role in the health-care continuum was vital. The day I started writing in a journal while in rehab, I was in physical therapy, and a young man was yelling at me, saying, "I won't let you give up." I had become fatigued, and my mind was unable to continue doing what he was asking of me. He wanted me to use a walker.

I yelled back, "How can I walk? I can't feel my feet."

He responded, "Get up and try."

Where did he go to school? I thought.

He was so nice, but he was yelling at me not to give up even when every part of my body had convinced my mind it was all right to do so.

He told me to focus on my sons and their faces and not on the task at hand, and that day my physical goals became very simple and clear. I was determined to walk again, even if it meant living with the constant numbness in my legs and feet. He believed in me. After several weeks of his pushing me to complete just one thing, I knew I wanted to change my life.

After several months in physical therapy, I felt a slight tingling in my feet, but only on occasion, which made standing or walking difficult. I just wanted to walk without having to stare at my feet to make sure they were still attached to my legs and without being afraid of falling. It didn't help that I had to wear a rigid plastic collar around my neck for months. It wasn't one of the soft foam ones—no, this thing around my neck was a rigid Aspen collar, and my neck underneath was horribly thin and white, like a chicken's neck or something out of a horror movie.

OCCUPATIONAL THERAPY

As I sat across from the occupational therapist one day, she calmly talked to me, trying to keep my mind occupied so I wouldn't notice as she dabbed my arm with an anesthetic and used tweezers to pull out shards of blue glass, which were embedded in the muscle and tissue of my right arm. This routine went on for a while: dabbing and pulling out glass, and then rebandaging my wounds, which were now just starting to heal. The injuries in my right arm had become severely infected just after the accident, which had caused a setback in the healing process; I had received IV antibiotics to stop the infection. During the accident, the side door had crumpled into me, and the glass had ripped the skin, tissue, and muscle away from the bone, which had to be reconstructed just after I arrived at the hospital. The healing process was triggering the glass to work its way through my muscle and skin to the top layer of skin; when it was touched, I felt the sharpness of the glass fragments.

By this point, the stitches from my right armpit down to my wrist had dissolved. But the deep scar will never disappear and will always remind me of that awful day. I had no feeling in my arm, no tingling, no sensation, nothing, so it didn't hurt. I glanced in the direction of the occupational therapist as she pulled several half-inch shards of blue glass from my forearm and wrapped them in gauze. I was shocked yet thankful that I couldn't feel anything.

The next day, a dermatologist came to my room. He checked the scars on my chin and left eye, where I had received more than twenty stitches, and verified that the wounds were healing. I was horrified to learn that the wound on my chin was infected and was reopening. The doctor saw a piece of blue glass inside the formerly completely healed tissue. *Here we go again,* I thought as he numbed my chin and used a magnifying glass as he pulled a jagged one-inch shard of window glass from my face. I was bleeding every-where, soaking bandages with blood as fast as he could replace them, before he could stitch and cover my wound yet again.

For some reason, I asked the doctor if I could keep that one jagged piece of glass. Looking at me strangely, he replied, "Are you sure?" By now I was overwhelmed by being poked and prod-ded, bleeding from various areas of my body, being wheeled in a wheelchair to rehab, and hearing patients in other rooms crying. Maybe I just wanted one simple thing that was causing me pain that I could identify with.

THE SCREAMING

Rehab was awful. The patient next door screamed every day, all day, because he had severe burns all over his body. His life had been spared, just like mine, but he was screaming in pain. His name was Jason, and he was a young father of three and had passed out with a cigarette, only to be awakened engulfed in flames. His body had to be scrubbed daily with a brush; I think it was to get the burned skin off his limbs. I saw his wife as she leaned against the hallway outside our adjacent rooms, crying while he screamed. This went on for hours, only to be repeated the next day. One day, while I was sitting in bed, feeling sorry for myself, she leaned in and smiled. "He'll be OK," I told her.

She replied, "We have three little girls at home. The youngest is four months old."

All I could do was remind her, "He'll be OK."

The elderly lady in the next bed finally went home, and I was happy for her—and also happy for myself because she snored all night, and I was barely able to sleep with her in the same room. I think this place was a vacation spot for her; she loved the attention she received. While I was happy to finally have some quiet time, it didn't last long. The next day, while I was in physical therapy, they brought in a young lady around nineteen or twenty years old. She'd had both arms amputated after a car accident and had a small baby. *Wow!* I thought. *Here I am complaining that I can't feel my feet, and she's a single mother who has no arms to hold her infant.* Well, that night was probably the worst night yet. Hearing her cry all night in pain was overwhelming, to say the least, and being in the same room with her didn't help the emotional and mental anguish I was going through.

I wanted to console her, because her life was now going to be different. How would she take care of a baby alone, with no husband and no arms? In a strange way, her hysterics all night and day allowed me to thank God for my injuries, and I prayed for her strength and mine. Then the emotions came rushing back in, and it became easier to just sleep. Sleep came easier and easier, because it was my only way to feel nothing.

Whenever I did finally fall asleep, my mind continued to race with the visions of my husband's brown eyes as he stared at me, reaching for me to hold on and save him. These visions were always accompanied by the sounds of the helicopter blades whipping around and around, and then nothing. The recurring sound in my head made sleeping almost impossible. It was similar to when someone is on a boat or roller coaster and is still able to feel the motion after getting off.

Realizing now that I was the last person my husband saw before he was pulled out of the van was powerfully disturbing, because I couldn't save him. So was the thought of his sudden fear, which was apparent in his eyes, of knowing that the life he knew would be gone forever. Was he aware he would never be able to hold his daughter from a previous marriage, watch her graduate and get married, or lead a normal life? These daily thoughts, sounds, and visions made any rational thoughts of normalcy completely disappear.

BATTLING DEPRESSION

As the weeks passed, my doctor asked the big question of how I felt. Suddenly a rush of tears came out, and I admitted I was sinking into a deep depression, with feelings of guilt and anger regarding an accident that I had no control over but that changed so many lives forever. I hated that I was a survivor; I told my doctor I couldn't live like this anymore. The physical pain and emotional ups and downs were a never-ending cycle, and I needed it to stop.

He advised me that I was experiencing PTSD and needed some help. I was grateful to him for saying that it was OK to feel this way. After several months of being on a mild medication and talking to a therapist, I started to feel somewhat normal again. This was a burden I carried on my own, without my sons knowing the emotional pain I was in.

I'd been on autopilot for so long that I'd forgotten to breathe. I just kept on going until one day it became my normal routine to keep my mind busy and not think, especially because I was so afraid I would slip back into that dark place within my own mind. My best friend, Donna, reminded me almost daily to put one foot in front of the other and breathe in and breathe out. "Well, that's a warm and fuzzy idea," I'd instinctively reply, "but what if your feet are in a constant state of tingling or have no feeling at all?"

The first few weeks after the accident were a complete blur. I guess the body has a way of healing itself by shutting down the brain or memories that are harmful to the body.

It was so surreal not knowing what was happening to me. This was the only time in my entire life that I didn't care about anything. As a mother who loves her sons more than life itself, I was angry that I wasn't there for them and that they had to grow up so fast, especially my older son, Brian. At some point he became the worrying parent watching out for his mother. How horrible could I have been not to care about my sons while I was recovering? I've devoted my life to being a great mother, and I've carried guilt deep down within me all these years because I wasn't there for my sons for a while. During my time in rehab, I heard that others were there for my sons when I wasn't able to be. Brian was dating a nice girl, April, whom he later married. Her parents came over to the house and cut the grass and brought food for them. I'll always appreciate these simple kindly gestures.

After I was released from rehab, I knew things would become difficult now, and I had to take control of my life and move on from a past I regretted. This was much easier said than done, and I realized I could keep busy but couldn't control my thoughts. The simple words "I'm moving on" became the words I muttered to myself on a daily basis.

During the initial weeks after my release, I had several moments when I thought I couldn't go on. I was still trying to deal with the residual effects of an accident that had changed my life and affected my health, with pounding headaches, lack of feeling in both feet, and muscle spasms in my neck and surrounding tissue. The numbness was so severe at times that I was unable to place one foot in front of the other, and the horrible spasms in my neck were so bad that I often vomited. The three-inch scar that hid the titanium in my fractured neck was tender, and the hypersensitivity of the large scar from the thirty or so stitches, slightly hidden beneath my hair, continues to this day. During these times I'd lie staring at the ceiling, wondering what was I going to do next. As I thought about those who took care of me in the hospital and during my rehabilitation, it hit me: I decided I wanted to start a business to give back and help others—a business that would change many lives.

CONCLUDING THOUGHT

External wounds may heal, but the real healing begins internally, starting with the mind, because if the mind isn't at peace, the rationalization of injuries becomes distorted, and the healing process slows.

"The Lord gives strength to those who are weary. Even young people get tired, then stumble and fall, but those who trust the Lord will find new strength. They will be strong like eagles; soaring upward on wings they will walk and run without getting tired" (Isa. 40:29–31, CEV).

CHAPTER 4

I'M MOVING ON

DECIDING MY PATH

Several months after leaving the rehabilitation facility, when I was still healing and suffering from devastating migraines that lasted several hours almost daily, I felt I had survived the accident so that I could do something more with my life, but I wasn't sure what. I felt it had something to do with the nurses and physical therapists who had helped me so much in those dark days.

What should I do? Some of my friends suggested I might see a therapist to help with my recovery and sorting out these life questions. I joked that writing was cheaper than visiting a therapist every day. Therapists listen to you talk, while writing allows you to form your thoughts on paper. So I began a journal.

Initially, these daily writings were more like a conversation with myself about how I felt each day and what I should do with my life. But gradually they developed into ideas and strategies and then a business plan. At first I wondered what I could offer single mothers like me seeking to make their families' lives better. Perhaps I could empower them to make a difference.

Suddenly I realized I was gravitating toward creating some kind of educational institution.

I wanted to start a college. I wanted to start a college that would be equal to a community college, but I only had basic business experience, and since I was an autodidact, all of it was self-taught. I had no formal college education, no nursing degree, and no MBA or PhD—what person in his or her right mind would want to start a college from nothing but determination?

I loved the idea of helping people develop skills that would be with them for a lifetime, and from my personal experiences as a patient, I knew nursing and physical therapy would always be careers that offered employment opportunities. So I felt education would be the way to help people acquire these skills. But I was now thirty-nine years old. I didn't feel the need to go to school to get an educational credential, especially since I'd gotten this far without any postsecondary schooling. Instead I wanted to do something bigger, something with the potential to change many lives. What could I do?

I read numerous books about colleges and universities and how they were founded. Then I researched the different types of strategic plans that schools use to develop their businesses. After a while I began writing my own plan, building on my notes that I had jotted down during my time in rehabilitation. But I often found myself discouraged, thinking, *I can't pull this off.* So I'd throw away everything I had written and start all over again. All this reading, researching, and writing helped keep my mind busy, so I didn't think about what could have been if I hadn't been in the accident that nearly killed me.

At times I struggled with my thoughts as they ran in various directions at the same time. On the one hand, I knew what I wanted to do, but on the other, I felt as if I were dreaming the impossible dream. How would I accomplish my dream? How would I help others change their lives? I thought, *I'm only one woman, struggling with mental, emotional, and physical injuries resulting from my accident. So why am I so obsessively focused on doing something so much bigger?* I also felt very alone. Though my two sons, Brian and Branden, believed in me, they were only eleven and sixteen years old. I felt I had no one to motivate me or tell me they were proud of me.

Then a good friend, Terrell, my accountant, gave me encouragement to continue. He told me, "I believe in you, and I'm not going to let you give up." His words gave me the strength to go on—and to this day, I'll never forget the encouragement of that simple statement. He also inspired me when I would call him, crying, telling him I was unsure of what to do next. He would calmly listen, and in his reassuring voice, he'd remind me, "You'll be fine." This was a gift to me, letting me know I wasn't alone and someone believed in me. Terrell's support gave me the confidence and impetus to go on.

STARTING A SCHOOL

Finally, inspired by everything I'd been through, I now knew what my purpose was. I was going to create a college to train nurses and physical therapists. I soon realized, however, that I needed the approval of the Florida Department of Education and the state board of nursing to go ahead with these plans.

In spring 2003, I began writing applications and stayed up many nights for months to make sure they were just right. I wanted to make the applications convincing, since this would be a new-school application, and I had little formal education myself. The two boards would need to know from my application that I had what it took to make the school a success. At times I was so obsessively and vigorously focused on completing these applications so they would be perfect that this process overcame my daily thoughts about anything else. This extreme dedication to perfection is an example of what happens when one has a type-A, obsessive-compulsive, overanalytical personality, just as the guidance counselors in grade school labeled me—though in this case, my approach eventually worked.

Meanwhile, as I worked on the application process, I was still managing my small medical-uniform business, which was housed in a shopping plaza. At the time it had a twenty-by-thirty-foot room that was used for storage. I hired someone to come and turn this empty space into a classroom by painting the walls and setting up ten used tables and twenty chairs. Nearby was another small room that I used as an office for the uniform business, where I had a desk, chair, and small bookcase. So now this small room became the office for the school too. While doing the initial research on creating a nursing program, I first had to understand the acronyms and complex words that identified every aspect of the human body. I had to understand what the words *GU, GI, integumental, respiratory,* and *neurology* meant, along with the other complicated terms that identify each body system.

After staying up all night and reading several chapters in the surgical book that identified the GU system (also known as the "genitourinary system"), I realized the complexity of each topic I was reading about—such as urinary cancer, physical abnormalities, and medications—was overwhelming. Then I had to learn about the central nervous system, neurological system, and respiratory and circulatory systems, to name a few, and how each body system relates to the others. After I learned about several systems, I had to tie the pharmacological aspect and contraindications and laboratory values into each one, followed by the diagnostic tests and treatments associated with each aspect of the disease process. Then let's not forget the medications used for each disease and diagnosis, and then came anatomy and physiology, and I had to learn about the muscles, bones, and joints.

During this time I fully understood how complex the injuries to my arm were. I pulled out the 2,900-plus pages of medical records from when I was hospitalized and compared my lab values with those identified in my studies as normal or abnormal. I discovered the process that takes place when someone codes, the medications given, and the techniques of resuscitation. I used my personal experience and medical records to comprehend the human body systems and my treatment plan for a head injury and fractured vertebrae. I learned how complex the medical charting process is and why.

I read every page of my personal medical file and absorbed in detail exactly when my heart stopped beating and for how long. Reading became my personal therapy, my refuge from the injuries from which I still suffered.

During my research in microbiology, I read several chapters on microorganisms and then watched a video of a fetal pig heart being dissected. The instructor sliced the little pig's heart in half, poking at the chambers while explaining how the blood flows. Then he stuck his finger into one of the small heart chambers and shook this little heart in the air at a student. I realized I needed to stop watching, or I would throw up.

When I turned to chapter nine in the surgical book, I saw graphic pictures of various stages of a decubitus ulcer, a wound usually found in the coccyx, the bony prominence where a patient sits and which can cause pressure when one lies down in one position for any length of time. I can tell you how to stage a wound based on its size in centimeters and the depth of tunneling, which means the wound isn't only deep but also trails off into a tunnel within the muscle, sometimes exposing the bone itself. In this case the wound must be packed to allow healing from within, and every time a bandage is removed from a decubitus ulcer, it also removes healthy skin tissue.

Can you imagine someone who isn't a nurse or a nursing student reading about oozing wounds with graphic pictures of open sores, some large enough that you could place your closed fist inside the wound? One picture showed a patient in poor living conditions with maggots crawling inside the wound. One day I met a friend for lunch at a restaurant. I explained in detail what I had just read, unaware that an elderly couple directly behind was eaves-dropping and listening to every disgusting word I was saying. The waitress came over and said, "Can you please not talk about bed-sores? You're grossing out the customers at the table next to you." I knew then that we were going to torture our nursing students with weak stomachs while we taught this material because of the disgusting things nurses have to deal with. At that moment I also realized the respect I have for the nursing profession.

While doing research in psychiatry, I read everything I could on OCD, ADD, and other acronyms for extremely obsessive peo-ple, along with what causes insomnia, nausea, hives, and emotion-al outbursts. I was confident I could diagnose anyone and probably even myself. I even observed our dog and diagnosed him as having OCD and anxiety disorder brought on by loud noises.

It was important to learn everything about the body to prepare myself for writing a college-level nursing-program curriculum. *Great*, I thought. *Now I have some understanding of the human body.* I felt prepared to start writing a nursing curriculum, but boy was I mistaken—not everyone can write a college nursing curriculum, especially if he or she has no knowledge of medicine or health care and passes out at the sight of blood. So I had to dig deeper and do more research.

I had to locate a curriculum framework in which to develop a pro-gram. I needed a template to identify each area necessary to de-velop a curriculum, so I started with the basics of each course. I had to develop daily lesson plans, including the delivery methods, and identify simple-to-complex lecture topics so students would understand the basics, and then transition into the more detailed areas, which eventually would help them develop strong critical-thinking processes.

After several months of research and development, I was fi-nally finished writing a college nursing curriculum that eventually would be used to train licensed practical nurses and registered nurses. *Wow, I did it*, I thought. Now I had to compile all the necessary information for a program application to the state nursing board. The data required was in-depth and addressed faculty, policies and procedures, job descriptions, nursing books, library resources, and each piece of equipment necessary to train nurses.

I was required to submit three identical copies of the same application. As I completed each section of the application, I chronologically organized the sections into the two binders that held each application, each one being more than four hundred pages long.

I also had to think about books for the school library. I started off with fifteen books on health care and medical procedures, which I had obtained from friends. This obviously wasn't enough for a school library, so I went to used bookstores, where I purchased every book I could find on medicine, surgery, pharmacology, nutrition, growth and development, childbirth, and nursing skills. One of the books even had someone's notes scrawled on each page with yellow highlighting.

I recruited my friends to help in the search, and a few days later, one of them found more books. Then others found still more books. And sometimes my book search scored big, like the one day when I went to a bookstore in St. Augustine. When I asked the elderly man at the counter about books on nursing, he showed me two boxes of books on every topic of health care. A nurse who was retiring had brought them in. I was ecstatic, feeling I had hit the jackpot.

"That's wonderful," I told him and eagerly handed him my five-dollar bill for both boxes.

I was so excited and eager to get the books home that I didn't even open the boxes. Later, when I looked through the boxes, I noticed that many of the books dated back to 1987—that must have been the year when the nurse who sold the books graduated. But at least most of the methods and techniques described in these books were still in use today. The pharmacology was more than likely outdated, but that didn't matter; I needed books to fill shelves, and now I had them.

I had close to fifty books, and now my library was ready. Meanwhile, as I waited for the approval from the state nursing board to come through, my friend Donna and I set up the other facilities that the school would need, even while these rooms continued to house the uniform business.

For example, the reception area to the uniform shop now became a place to buy uniforms as well as get supplies for school. One section sold drawstring pants and nursing shoes, while another section featured a long clothing rack with blue and pink scrub tops. Nearby were two small dressing rooms with curtains. To enable students to take tests in these dressing rooms, I took two overbed tables, which are placed in front of patients for meals, from two hospital beds in the school's skills laboratory and placed them, along with a folding chair, in each dressing room. This way a student would go in to take a test, and afterward someone could use this same room to try on uniforms.

In addition, next to the reception area, I set up a small room with two hospital beds, overbed tables, walkers, a pole for IV equipment, a wheelchair, and other medical equipment that I purchased at yard sales. This area was designed to be a kind of lab room where students could practice different nursing skills, such as giving bed baths, transferring patients from a bed to a chair, and helping patients use a bedside commode.

Initially, the classroom and laboratory doors were left open for the students to have easy access. But then an incident led me to keep the doors tightly closed. A young lady came into the store to try on uniforms, and she brought her toddler. As she paid for her purchases, her son ran around at her feet and then disappeared. We nervously looked around for him for a few minutes. Then he suddenly yelled, "Mama! Mama!" The woman ran toward the sound of his shouts and finally found him in my makeshift skills laboratory, where he was sitting on a bedside commode next to a bed. "Look, Mama," he said proudly, "I went poop"—and so he had.

Another challenge we faced in these early days was that the Department of Education and board of nursing required schools to have a break room for students. But the rented location didn't have enough rooms, so I decided to use the back of the building, which had a loading dock. It had concrete block walls and very large double doors, which swung wide open to reveal an eight-foot drop to the ground. It was designed so trucks could pull up to unload a shipment to the dock.

Though it was plain, with painted concrete block walls, it provided the space we needed to make students comfortable while taking their breaks. I bought two square folding tables and four chairs for each of them. I placed these tables and chairs next to the concrete block wall and adjacent to a sheet of plywood that was supported by a small cabinet on each side and had a plastic sheet to cover the wood. Then, underneath the plywood, I placed a three-foot fridge and storage bins with extra uniforms, since this was the only storage area I had available. So now I had a makeshift kitchen that the students could use during their breaks. The downside of this arrangement was that in the summertime it became very hot in the back area because it had no air-conditioning, so the double doors that led to the loading dock remained open all day long.

While the back of the building still looked like a warehouse despite these additions, turning it into an area for breaks was at least a start. I had just the bare bones set up to gain the necessary approvals from the Department of Education.

I still had to go through a site visit by the board of nursing to verify that we had the necessary space and equipment. On the day of the visit, a lady walked in after traveling from Tallahassee. She began by walking around and looking at the variety of shoes and uniforms hanging on the uniform rack, and then she walked into our classroom and skills laboratory, taking notes the whole time. Inside the skills laboratory, she commented that the equipment was old and obviously well used, and she observed that the library books were older than the ones she had used when she was in school for nursing. Her final stop was the student lounge; we walked through the heavy sliding doors that separated the front air-conditioned area from the rear loading dock, which wasn't insulated and had no air-conditioning vents.

She sat down at the card table so we could talk about our visit results, which would be a big factor in gaining approval from the board of nursing. As soon as she sat down, a swarm of wasps flew out from under our fold-up table, and several stung her. "Oh, my gosh!" she cried out. "I'm allergic to wasps!"

She grabbed her purse and stuck herself with an EpiPen to prevent an allergic reaction. Apologizing repeatedly, I realized the wasps must have come in the day before while the doors were open, and when I closed up, they'd been trapped inside. As she left, I worried about her report on our facilities, especially in light of the wasp attack.

The day I went before the board, I was very nervous, because I knew her report was going to be a topic of discussion. It was only a few months after my accident, and I felt like a boot-camp soldier trying to climb over an enormous wall in a hot jungle. I was still unsteady on my feet, which were constantly numb. My weight was well below a hundred pounds, and I still suffered from severe dizziness, which caused me to easily fall. Though I was supposed to wear a rigid brace to support my neck, I refused to do so. I was also supposed to walk with the assistance of a walker but refused to do that as well, fearing humiliation as I walked down the long aisle past hundreds of onlookers. I'd already been through hell and feared they might judge me.

To make matters worse, the day before I went before the board of nursing, I learned that the director of the nursing program was prepared to speak on behalf of the community college to the full board to express her disapproval of our receiving program approval. The next day, when I appeared before the board, which consisted of six registered nurses, all holding various levels of nursing degrees and employment titles, I felt as if I looked like I was 150 years old and had just been dug up from my final resting place. As I walked into the large room and waited for my name to be called, I was wearing two layers of clothing, with a sweater under my jacket and sweatpants under a larger size of pants. I was embarrassed that I looked so sickly and didn't want my overly thin appearance to detract from my presentation. I wanted to let the board know I had prepared a solid nursing application and curriculum, as well as procedures, marketing materials, and lesson plans, that I had selected the appropriate books for each course, and that I had a strong business model.

Suddenly, my name was called. As I walked in front of the board members, each person stared at me like scholars passing judgment on a misbehaving student. As I stood in front of them, I felt as though they didn't have any sympathy for what I had experienced while recovering from my accident—and how could they? I'd never informed them of what I'd gone through or what had inspired me to start a school for nursing. They were only judging me on my application, which took months of research and hard work to develop and which I'd compiled with several thousand pages of perfected details to show I had successfully submitted a strong nursing program application that met all their requirements.

I was scared and nervous, imagining how others in a similar situation must have felt when they gave their all to a project, tirelessly working for months or years to bring it to fruition, and then faced a time of judgment, knowing that a select few men and women with large egos and attitudes to match could squash their dreams in a second by saying no. Now, for me, it was that judgment day, and it all came down to the board members' idiosyncratic opinions or interpretations of what they thought the board of nursing rules were or should be.

Finally, after the panel asked me about twenty questions, and I was about to hear my fate, the panel moderator asked everyone in the audience, "Does anyone have objections to this nursing school being approved?"

I was stunned by this announcement, since I'd already completed and submitted each application section, and now the panel was opening up the approval process to more possible objections.

An older woman who looked and dressed like the cartoon character Olive Oyl slowly walked up the aisle to the long table next to where I sat and proceeded to sit next to me. She introduced herself as the director of the nursing program at our local community college and stated to every board member, along with several hundred onlookers, those from other schools and colleges, and everyone else sitting in the audience, "Nursing programs shouldn't be taught at private schools. Only community colleges and universities should be allowed to train nurses." Then she continued firmly, "Students won't get a good education at this school."

I got very angry and thought, *Here we go again.* My inner demons of anger rose strongly; I felt I had no control over this anger that was compelling me to do something to fight back.

Finally, driven by my anger after listening intently and struggling to keep my composure, I reached over and handed her a business card. As I did, I smiled with an otherwise emotionless poker face, as if I had plastered a smile over my seething but hidden fury, and told her, "Call me if I can ever do anything for you."

In response she glared at me with what seemed like venom in her soul. She seemed to have so much anger toward me and my efforts to build a nursing school in our community. Why? I believed she hoped to destroy my school because of her own personal reasons and resentments—or was she threatened by me?

On that day I vowed that I'd never give up on the employees and students who depended on me. In fact, in response to this women's hatred, I asked myself, *What would God want me to do?*

After the woman's comments, the board members began to deliberate as if I were on trial for murder, and I anxiously awaited their answer.

Finally, the verdict came down. The panel moderator turned to me and said, "Congratulations. We've decided to approve your application for a nursing program. We wish you much success as you educate nurses."

I was happily amazed. Somehow I had managed to get the board of nursing's approval for our school to offer a licensed practical nurse (LPN) degree.

The answer came back loud and clear: "Continue to work to make the school a success, and don't let others stand in your way." After that, I made another vow to myself that I should never talk down about other people; rather, I should lift them up by praying for them to find their own way. It was as if the board's approval helped affirm my belief that this was my purpose for surviving that tragic day, and I was determined to make this purpose happen. Despite my physical pain, I had to push through.

My appearance before the board was also my first truly meaningful experience regarding the importance of not giving up. So from that day on, if someone said to me, "You can't do that," my response was always, "Hold on tight and watch me." As I came to realize that day, you've got to have the passion not to let anyone or anything stop you. In fact, I sometimes thought of myself as a train going full speed downhill, knowing that nothing could stop me except God. And by seeing my determination, no one would want to make me put on the brakes to stop.

After gaining the board's approval, I could move forward by putting that bad experience with the older woman, along with my feelings of anger, behind me. My experience in front of the board also reminded me that I had stepped out in faith to establish my school, which was something nearly everyone at the time had said was impossible. But now I realized again that if you have faith and a true belief in your abilities, you can accomplish anything. The woman at the board meeting had tried to throw me off my path with her anger, but I had stood up to her and resolved to continue to make my school even stronger. The experience helped me recommit to my purpose and move on in that spirit. It's like the popular saying goes, "What doesn't kill you makes you stronger," though in this case it was an angry competitor who hoped to kill my school and my dreams.

The next approval was from the Department of Education; the application process was as in-depth, but I applied the same determination as with the nursing board. On the day I was to present the new school application, I sat there waiting for my name to be called, and it was. Only this time, I did not have to feel intimidated or defensive. The board chair called my name and immediately said, "No need to stand up; your application for a new nursing school has been approved. Congratulations."

RECRUITING STUDENTS

Now that I had the facilities set up and the approval of the board of nurses, the next step was getting students to enroll. In the spirit of the *Field of Dreams* mantra, I thought, *If you build it, they will come.* We had built the school, so now the question was, how would we let the prospective students know it was open?

To this end I began our recruitment campaign, although I had no money for advertising. Instead, I sent out hundreds of faxes to prospective students, using a list of numbers I'd received from hospital physician directories and the nearby chambers of commerce. I also went to every health and vendor fair in the area, and I collected fax numbers from every business card I could obtain at these events.

Then, at a time before the Internet made it possible to send out e-mail blasts to hundreds or thousands of people, I recruited my seventy-five-year-old mother to send out the faxes, which had to be sent individually. To do so, she sat in front of the fax machine, punching in each fax number to send out the faxes one at a time. The fax announced that the new school was "Now Enrolling, Practical Nursing Program Starting Soon." The fax announcement concluded with an invitation to attend our open house.

Once this first wave of potential recruits received the faxes, they spread the word to their friends, who in turn contacted their friends. Our marketing efforts turned into a huge success, since a great many of those who received our faxes turned our enrollment invitation into a word-of-mouth message spread in person or by telephone. It was an approach that worked quickly, at a time before cell phones, Twitter, Facebook, and mobile apps were used for spreading messages. One of the reasons this approach worked so well was that the message was one many students were eager to hear, because they'd been waiting for one or two years for acceptance into the nursing program of the competitor who had tried to prevent our program from receiving approval. This competing school had only a small number of openings each year, so applicants were placed on a long waiting list.

Within a few weeks, we had more than three hundred applicants for a place in our first classroom, which could hold up to twenty-four students. We held an informational session for those who were interested, which looked like a concert in the park, since we had so many people show up. They parked on the grass or down the street, and because our building wasn't that big, not everyone could get in at the same time. A long line of prospective students waited outside for someone to leave so they could go in.

I was immediately heartened by the overwhelming response to our marketing efforts, which, as I mentioned, cost the school nothing because we had no money to advertise. The enthusiasm of the attendees at our informational session was a sign that I was on the right track in providing training that was wanted and needed by so many.

For example, a single mom who was on welfare told me she had been waiting for two years for acceptance into nursing school, and she desperately wanted to get into our program, since she wanted a better life for her children. When she came into my office, I noticed she was very heavy and could barely squeeze into the chair in front of me. Then she pulled out a letter she had received from a local community college and begged me to accept her.

"I was denied admission to their program," she explained, "because they said I'd be unable to handle the physical limitations of nursing."

"What limitations are you talking about?" I asked.

"Well, the director told me my weight was a factor," she said. "But I really want to do this. I very much want to become a nurse."

I was sure she weighed more than four hundred pounds, but I saw that her passion for the profession was there.

"OK," I said. Then I got up, walked around the desk, bent down, and hugged her. "Just pass the entrance exam, and you're in."

Her face lit up with excitement because I'd given her a chance.

Later, when she passed the exam, I complimented her and told her I was proud of her. One year later, she graduated from our program and is still working as a nurse today.

Stories like this helped me see how badly our school was needed, and they reminded me that it isn't just grades, book learning, and conformity to preset criteria that make a good nurse; rather, it's having passion to become a nurse, along with committing to lifelong learning and developing the skills and knowledge to do well in school and later become successful in the profession.

THE FIRST YEAR

During this first year, which was taught over twelve months with no breaks except for the usual holidays, we enrolled twenty-four students for each day and evening class, with each course running directly after the other. Our instructors weren't initially trained as instructors with education credentials, but all of them were registered nurses. I had to set up a "train the trainer" program to help them build up competence as educators. This was far more difficult than any application process, because again I had no formal training to develop an educator program, and this training was typically completed by nurses with a master's degree.

It was inspiring to see all these students arrive eager to learn from the health practitioners who led the classes, which provided not only academic training about the principles of nursing but also the lab and clinical skills necessary to take care of patients. The curriculum was designed to develop a student's ability to understand the wide range of nursing theory. This included applying critical-thinking processes, which means one doesn't just rely on set answers but works out the solution to a problem when needed—an approach that's very difficult for the average person to comprehend.

In determining the particular courses to teach, I set up the program in keeping with the nursing board's guidelines regarding what we were required to teach, which included every aspect of the health-care system, along with particular diseases and bodily functions. This included the respiratory, integumental, GI, GU, reproductive, and neurological processes. We also taught ethics, nursing theories, the Nurse Practice Act, and medication administration. I was especially focused on offering a program that emphasized day-to-day practices, along with the importance of being caring and compassionate to patients. This is what the nurses would experience every day on the job, just as I had experienced that care and compassion from the therapists and nurses who treated me.

EXPANDING THE SCHOOL

By the end of the first year, we had enrolled forty-eight students who would be expected to graduate in twelve months, and we still had more than two hundred applications from students who wanted to attend. Since we had so many students seeking admittance, it was obvious that we needed to secure a larger location, not only to serve our current students but also to enroll even more students in classes in the following years. I was already dreaming big, imagining how the school could serve thousands of students.

After spending the next few months looking around our small town, I finally found the perfect building: a three-bedroom house with a full kitchen, walk-in closets, and full bathrooms, which previously had been the model home for a new real-estate development. The interior of the house was painted with beige walls and trim, which was a nice, subdued color for a school setting, but outside the lawn was brown and dead. It clearly hadn't been watered in months, and there was no landscaping. I immediately thought of how the exterior could be revitalized with attractive plantings of shrubs and flowers.

After renting the building, I decided to use the large living room in front as the main office and reception area. I took over the master bedroom for my office and found the master shower ideal for storing supplies. I also turned the large walk-in closet into a storage area for the telephone system and several changes of clothes, because one evening I'd fallen asleep in the skills laboratory on a hospital bed, only to wake up when several students walked into the room. I sleepily greeted them with some embarrassment. I thought the other two bedrooms were ideal for small offices. In the reception area, I placed a desk, a copy machine, chairs, and a larger table, where students could fill out applications.

There was also a second building behind the house that had a forty-by-fifty-foot room, which would make a great classroom, and also one bathroom. Plus it had an adjacent large room with another bathroom that we could use as a skills laboratory and two ten-by-ten-foot rooms near that, which I thought would be ideal for a student lounge and an instructor's office.

Since the school desperately needed a larger library of nursing books, I went back to every flea market and yard sale in the area and purchased as many used nursing books as I could. Soon the shelves were filled with hundreds of nursing books, manuals, and periodicals. Students could read them there or borrow them, in addition to buying their own books from a local bookstore.

It was heartening to see all the students enthusiastically pursue their courses and get to know one another. In these first years after our opening year, we graduated annually an average of sixty-five nurses, more than one hundred nursing assistants, and fifty or so home health aides, as well as nearly sixty CPR students each week—all in a single classroom, with one employee scheduling classes during the day, evening, and on weekends. At least this single classroom was much larger than the room in our first building, with the school being based in the same building as my uniform business, which I had phased out and closed. This larger space allowed us to grow—and that was just the beginning. I was determined to see the school grow even larger.

BECOMING AN ACCREDITED COLLEGE

Now that the school was on its feet and growing, I decided it was time to start the accreditation process, since being accredited would give the school more credibility and help students find jobs. To that end I spent more than a year developing policies, procedures, and plans to align our programs and every aspect of the school with the standards of excellence needed to achieve accreditation. This process was tedious and at times overwhelming, but it was necessary, though each step to achieve this prestigious title was more complex than the one before. It was a major challenge to meet all the requirements, since accreditation applications are much more detailed than an application to the board of nursing or Department of Education. And to provide the required answers, I needed to carefully review the standards to decipher what the accreditor wanted the school to provide and to express them in clear terms, though in elegant, formal language to show well-thought-out planning and erudition.

I knew it was crucial to achieve this accreditation, since this regulatory approval is necessary for many things, including students being able to secure jobs in the future. I also wanted the accreditation so I could say to our students and the community, as well as to my competitor, that we were delivering a quality education. Later, after receiving full accreditation, I wanted to send a copy to the director of nursing at the local community college who had been so critical about the success of our school. I wanted to show her we had done it, as a kind of "in your face" gesture.

As part of the accreditation process, I attended several regulatory meetings to learn about the latest requirements. These meetings were informative and provided a good source of contacts with other educators. They also were something of an eye-opener regarding the attitudes that some male educators still held about women in top jobs in the nursing field. These men were like dinosaurs, harking back to a time when higher education was a sinecure for male administrators.

For example, at one meeting I overheard several male school owners and campus presidents talking. Suddenly one gentleman looked in my direction and asked me, "Who started your school?"

I smiled proudly and replied, "I did."

He looked at me quizzically, his eyebrows raised as if he thought I was kidding. He continued, "No, really, who's the owner? You should be at home with your kids."

"I really am the founder and CEO," I told him.

He looked appropriately chagrined by my comeback. "Oh, I'm sorry," he said. "I hope I didn't offend you."

This experience made me realize how far women still have to go to get full acceptance in an educational industry that traditionally has had male leadership. But I was glad to be one of those leading the way, and I felt my ability to do this was an example of how much women could do to get ahead if only they set their minds to it.

A FLOOD IN MY OFFICE

We were preparing for submitting a new program application to the nursing board, and I desperately needed table space, but our offices were so small. So I used what was available: the floor. I had five three-ring binders filled with detailed syllabi, schedules, clinical contracts, faculty résumés, other contracts, book listings, and laboratory supply lists after lists after lists, and then Friday came. By this time, after working for three months on this application, we were done and ready to organize each pile into the appropriate tabs in the binders and express-mail them on Monday morning. We all went home exhausted to wait patiently until Monday morning. I had a great weekend, relaxing and having fun. On Monday, I pulled into work at the same time as another long-term employee, both of us laughing. I remember having a cup of coffee in my hand when I opened up the side door, only to have four feet of water come rushing out into the parking lot, along with every piece of paper I had organized so neatly on my office floor—which, by the way, was closed and locked. The water was so high, it had washed the trash out of the cans, and those too were in the yard.

The leak had apparently started sometime over the weekend from the kitchen fridge's ice-maker hose coming loose, falling off, and pouring out water. I had an open house scheduled a few days later, so we had to get out the water and dry the carpet and our documents. After several weeks of working with the doors wide open, the carpet started smelling musty, and I knew I had no other options. There were no other affordable buildings to rent on such short notice, so I sucked it up and cleaned the carpet myself. It took several weeks using a rented machine, pouring every logical solution into the scrubber, methodically going over every inch of carpet and then putting the air-conditioner as low as sixty degrees to remove the moisture. Eventually the smell was removed.

AN AGREEMENT

Another struggle I faced was getting a local hospital to accept our students. The struggle began soon after I received full accreditation for the school. A few days after I was notified that the school was fully accredited, I met with a department director of the local hospital about allowing our students to do a rotation there. At first he refused, but he wouldn't tell me why. A few days later, I received an official letter in the mail saying, "Approval for student rotation denied."

I was upset and then angry about these denials. Why wouldn't the hospital let my students participate in its rotation, which was crucial for them to get the hands-on experience they needed to succeed? So I began to randomly show up at the director's office and knock on the door in order to speak to him. Again and again he told me, "I'm sorry, but we can't discuss the reason for the denial."

I wouldn't take no for an answer. "I need an answer as to why you refused to allow our nursing students to practice in your hospital," I said, because this made no sense to me, since our school was accredited.

When the director again responded, "I can't tell you," I came back a week later and asked again. He echoed the same refrain: "I can't tell you." After several times repeating this same routine, I finally decided I was hitting a brick wall. So I decided to go to a higher level and sent a detailed letter to every member of the board of directors, every physician who had privileges at the hospital, every department head, and every local county commissioner, as well as the mayor of our town and several mayors in surrounding towns. The list included more than 120 people.

In my letter I explained that the hospital wouldn't let our students participate in the rotation as nurses in training. I also questioned why the hospital had paid more than $15,000 to bring one nurse from the Philippines to our area to work in the hospital when we had local graduates who were licensed nurses eager to work in their community. I also raised the question of why, since this was a public hospital, wasn't it supposed to meet the needs of the public?

I concluded by saying, "If our students are going to be denied participation in a clinical rotation at your hospital, I want to know what the hospital has against our students. We have more than fifteen of your hospital employees enrolled in our nursing program. So if we're good enough to train your staff, why aren't we good enough for you to allow them to do a rotation at your hospital?"

In addition to sending this letter, I asked all the employees who were our students to write letters of support requesting that they be able to do a rotation at the hospital that they worked at and loved. Also, to make my argument in the letter even stronger, I pointed out that every one of the hospital employees who was receiving an education at our college would acquire an excellent clinical experience at another local hospital, where we would encourage them to seek employment after graduation. If they didn't include our students in the clinical rotation, they could expect to lose their employees to the competition after they graduated with nursing degrees.

Within three days of sending out the letter, I received more than eighty phone calls from board members, doctors, hospital department heads, and government officials, all showing local support. I made a list of the callers and their contact information.

Finally, I received the one phone call I'd been waiting for from a hospital employee. Though she refused to tell me her name, she said, "You caused a stir, and everyone's talking about your letter and your school." I smiled hearing her say that people were talking about my small, privately owned nursing school.

Then she told me about the response I'd gotten from the local community college. "The same woman from the community college who showed up at the board of nursing meeting told the hospital that if they approved your nursing students, the college would remove every student from their hospital and never use them again."

When I heard that, I was appalled that a college would threaten us like this, since it was just me, one woman, fighting against a large community college. I didn't blame the hospital. I now understood its position, but again I felt as if I were fighting the big boys on the block, and I was determined not to lose.

The community's support behind me was so great, reflected in the outpouring of letters and phone calls I received from physicians and community members, that within three days the hospital changed its mind. As a result, I received what I'd been waiting eight years for: an agreement that my students would be accepted into the hospital's rotation program.

I felt gratified and validated for my persistence in fighting to get what I felt the students and my college deserved. We have a wonderful local hospital, and I knew our students could get a quality education, and that's all that I wanted—a chance for them to succeed by applying the skills they learned from our school in a good hospital setting.

BUILDING A COLLEGE CAMPUS

After another few years of our school being in two small buildings with only one large classroom, I wanted to help even more students. That meant I needed more programs and more classrooms. So I had to develop a strategic plan and timeline to identify which programs to offer, when to start, how much to charge, which policies to implement, and which supplies, equipment, and clinical sites would be needed so students could practice their skills on real patients. I also met with administrators, staff, and other decision-makers at additional hospitals to make arrangements so my school could send its students to their sites. Since we had grown so much, I realized we needed a larger building. But where should it be?

Just as I began thinking about where we could move, I found the perfect place while driving home from the bank. As I glanced to my right, I saw an empty lot and pulled off the side of the road to look closer. The lot was filled with large oak trees, and I was sure it would make a perfect picnic area for our students. It also looked like the ideal site for a larger school building, because it was located close to many restaurants and was on a corner lot. But mostly I liked it because I envisioned sitting under those large, beautiful trees.

I drove to the nursing college and excitedly got out of my car. Then I walked into our small office and announced, "I found the perfect place for our new campus."

The two employees working in the administrative office were similarly excited, and they asked me to take them to the site, assuming it already had a building. But when they got there, they were surprised.

"But there are only trees and dirt," one of them said, sounding shocked.

"Well, that's where we'll build our new college from the ground up," I said.

I spent the next year getting blueprints for the architect and going to bank after bank for financing, but it was a struggle due to my low credit score. I had paid my mortgage late for several months while I was in the rehabilitation facility after my accident. Then, to make matters worse, while completing an application for credit, I discovered I'd been a victim of identity theft.

"It looks like someone else used your personal information to spend more than four million dollars to buy homes, cars, and jewelry in Miami," the bank official said.

I hardly could believe it. I couldn't even get financing for one hundred dollars, let alone enough to build a college campus, and someone had used my information to spend a fortune. Not only was my credit already bad, but I also had to clean up the mess created by someone else before I could get a loan to build the new campus.

I had to spend several months proving that I was in fact who I said I was by going to the social security office and filing police reports. When I tried to find out more about the person who had used my identity, the bank refused to give me any further information. Just to take back my own identity, I had to go through a long process of proving I wasn't the person who had spent millions. Again and again, I had to provide different banks months of bank statements, credit-card receipts, and other personal information to prove that I wasn't the same person who had listed a man's name with my information and lived in Miami and that I hadn't defaulted on any loans. It was a bureaucratic nightmare.

Finally, after going through this process for months, I decided to contact a lawyer and go after the bank. I wanted it to be held accountable as coconspirator in the identity theft, because the theft had occurred due to one of its employees not doing due diligence in approving a big loan. My lawyer sent a very harsh letter to the bank, and to my surprise, the identity-theft problem was cleared up within a few days. The bank agreed to place a warning on my credit report to alert potential lenders that I had been the victim of identity theft.

Finally, that problem was cleared up as one more hurdle I'd been able to jump over. Soon afterward, I found someone to help me secure a USDA loan, though it was a long, tedious process. After several months, my application and supporting documents were in three two-inch binders, which contained an extensive history about the school—from every idea I had for creating it and where the school started to my ten-year detailed goals and strategies for our future.

This application process was where my being obsessively organized came in handy. Over the years I had developed detailed plans and steps to accomplish each of my goals and tasks, as well as a timeline for completing them. The result was a series of detailed books that described my goals and dreams, along with the chronological order in which different tasks to achieve them had been completed. Conveniently, I now had all these records of completion sitting in front of me in one place so I could readily review them.

Once I got the loan, I was excited that I had a chance for a new campus and new beginning. I hired a great local builder, an architect, and an engineer. Finally, my building was on its way.

It was exciting to see the building going up. Every day I drove by and stopped to walk around the property and building to see how things were going. The builder added walls, a roof, plumbing, blacktop for the driveway, and finally landscaping. After eight or so months, the building was completed, and it looked exactly as I had envisioned it.

Amazingly, I remember that first day of walking onto the campus as vividly as if it happened yesterday. I brought my dad to see the building. I was so excited and happy. Just as the installers were laying the tile flooring around the front double doors, my dad walked over, picked up a black marker, and decided to write his name on the concrete, so I sat down next to him and wrote mine too. Just below my name, I included the statement, "God's grace is unmerited favor." When I finished, I thought, *Wow! Our names are there forever as you enter the building. My statement is going to greet every person who enters those doors.* My school was now a home.

As I sat outside the building, reflecting on everything that had brought my small school to this large building and campus, my older son Brian walked up to me. Looking at me innocently, he said something I wasn't expecting: "Mom, I'm so proud of what you've accomplished." His words echoed through me, and I will never forget his sincerity.

For our grand opening, I invited a state representative who'd been a longtime friend to be our guest speaker, and I was honored when he agreed. When I first told him a few months after my accident, while I was still recovering, that I wanted to start a college, he became one of my earliest supporters. He told me back then, "You'll do anything you set your mind to. Don't let anyone stop you." So I thought it was fitting that he should be there to see the school's great growth, as shown in part by our new building.

The next day we were open for business in our new home. At last, as I stood there, I thought, *Now we look like a real school. We have all the licenses, and now we have a real campus.*

I reflected on how the school had grown over the years since I founded it, from nothing to a licensed, accredited college. And what a ride of transformation it had been. The process was a little like raising a child from infancy through the childhood years to adolescence and adulthood. Along the way, there had been so many stories: funny events, crazy students, and psycho instructors with strange eccentricities, though they never harmed anyone. It was wonderful to think about all these stories, like a parent recalling the milestones in the growth of her child.

I also realized that as my business grew and my ideas and decisions turned into realities while I overcame all sorts of obstacles, everything I had gone through had changed me. From an ordinary, carefree woman who just thought about how to have fun on the weekends, I had become a strong, confident businesswoman and developed a resilient sense of purpose and a will to make things happen. I was very pleased with the leader and the mentor I had become and the many students I had nurtured to secure fulfilling careers.

The following chapter is a collection of stories about the students and teachers who were part of the school, many of whom are still good friends of mine today.

CONCLUDING THOUGHT

Simple words of encouragement can mean the difference between success and failure. If someone fails at something, it doesn't define who that person is, unless he or she embraces failure as a way out. Pick yourself up, refocus, and try again.

"I have not yet reached my goal, and I am not perfect. But Christ has taken hold of me. So I keep on running and struggling to take hold of the prize.

My friends, I don't feel that I have already arrived. But I forget what is behind, and I struggle for what is ahead" (Phil. 3:12–13, CEV).

CHAPTER 5
STUDENT STORIES

As the college grew over thirteen years into an institution that now served more than three hundred students a year, I met many students who had their own stories. For example, some students were able to overcome crises in their personal lives and turn around lives filled with poverty, abuse, and other personal challenges to gain success in nursing careers. This chapter features some of the most interesting and inspirational stories.

As the days have turned into years, the memories of the inspiration I've received from students and faculty have become more valuable. I know the time I've spent with them has changed my life for the better. I've met a number of young men and women, many of whom come from poorer socioeconomic backgrounds, who are on autopilot in their lives. Many want something out of life and are willing to work hard to get it; they just need people to tell them how proud they are of them. Again, simple words of encouragement can mean the difference between success and failure. I've never accepted failure as a way out. Failure only means that a person may not be good at one thing or another. So I get in these young people's faces and remind them that others will respect them for failing; they just need to pick themselves up and try again.

I tell them that quitting is on the other side of success. If you quit when things get hard, you'll always be a quitter. So take a deep breath and set your plans, and when they're done, pat yourself on the back, since you just completed the first step to success.

A TALE OF TWO SISTERS

After we finally got approved and started our first nursing class, I prided myself on knowing every student's name. I had also met most of their family members and knew where the students worked. If students had difficult personal situations, I usually knew about them, and in many cases, I helped the students overcome their problems so they could complete their classes and graduate. But I was in for a rude awakening regarding how much I knew when I discovered some unexpected personal facts about two students.

One of the students—I'll call her Jill—was the life of the class, since she was always talking to everyone, and she set up some study groups so several students could study together. But the other student, whom I'll call Jessie, was standoffish, quiet, and self-reliant. Though Jill and Jessie were friends, they didn't seem to be close. They didn't talk to each other much at school, and Jessie didn't join any of Jill's study groups. But I thought that was fine, since both were very good students, and I enjoyed meeting with them at different times to learn about their progress at school.

Then, the following year, when both women were graduating, I made an unexpected discovery. This occurred at the graduation ceremony, when all the students had to write a few words expressing thanks to their mentors, families, and friends. First, Jill came up and read her speech, saying how nice it was that she had received her diploma, nursing pin, and cap, and how much she appreciated the help of her family and God in completing the program. Then she sat down—nothing unusual about that. Next, several other students came up one at a time when their names were called so they could read their personal thank-yous.

Finally, when Jessie came up, there was the big reveal. Like the other students, she began by thanking her family and God, but then she added, "And I want to thank my sister for being my study partner, friend, and classmate." It was a big shocker, because no one in the school, including me, realized Jill and Jessie were sisters, since one was married and had a different last name.

WHAT ONE STUDENT WILL DO TO GET OUT OF TAKING AN EXAM

I usually try to bend over backward to accommodate students when they face obstacles in their personal or family lives or difficult financial situations that interfere with their schoolwork, attendance, or final exams. I've granted extensions, given extra help, and otherwise tried to help committed students deal with these life problems so they can graduate and move on successfully with their careers.

But there was that one student who tried to take advantage of this policy by inventing a family tragedy that didn't really exist. That was what happened when a student I'll call Andrea told me her story. I initially had called her into my office because of her numerous absences. As she sat across from me, I explained why it was important to attend the scheduled classes.

"If you don't go to class, you won't learn what you need to learn to work as a nurse and be prepared to take your final exams," I told her.

In response, she explained in great detail how she couldn't take an upcoming exam at the scheduled time because of a tragedy in her family.

"Both my parents were killed in a car accident a few days ago," she told me.

Not only was she grieving, she said, but she also had to make their funeral arrangements.

"I'm so sorry about your loss," I told her and rescheduled her exam for two weeks later.

At once she was all smiles and tears as she effusively said, "Thank you so much for making this change."

I hugged her as she left the office, thinking how she needed this extra time to grieve and recover from the loss of her parents. I turned back to my desk to continue working, pleased that I could help another student.

A few hours later, I got a call from a student who told me, "I just heard Andrea bragging about getting out of taking an exam by telling you her parents were killed in an accident. But her parents are very much alive. A few of us were at their house studying last evening, and that's who's signing her tuition checks."

Stunned, I put down the phone. I went into the nursing school's office, found copies of past checks, and verified the names of Andrea's parents. Then I reviewed the footage from the video camera in the hallway near my office, which was mainly there for security in case of a break-in or burglary. When I rolled back the video to the time when Andrea had left the office, I saw her. She was right there, laughing and smiling, apparently unaware that she was on camera as she spoke to a few students and told them how she had avoided taking an exam she wasn't prepared to take. She was obviously pleased that she'd been able to get away with something.

I was shocked by what Andrea had done and how she seemed so blatantly prideful about it. I decided to confront her, and a few days later, I asked her to come into my office to discuss the exam. When she did, sitting at my desk across from me, I motioned for her parents to come into my office, since I had called them to confront Andrea with me. As soon as they appeared, the color in Andrea's face faded, her eyes wide open, staring at her parents.

"Oh, I called your parents to personally give them my apologies for missing their funeral," I told her with some irony. "And now here they are."

Andrea apologized for what she had done to both me and her parents. They told her how ashamed of her they were for lying to me. Again, she apologized profusely and promised never to lie again to her parents or to me. I relented and let her take the rescheduled exam. Subsequently, she passed her test and got her LPN license, and we became friends.

JUST NEEDED A RIDE

Sometimes all a student needs is a ride as a helping hand. That's what happened when I got a call from a student I'll call Marcus, a single father of four young children, just getting by on public assistance. He was determined to get through our LPN program to become a nurse so he could reverse his fortune and support his kids.

One Friday in fall 2005 at 6:45 a.m., I got a frantic call from Marcus on my personal cell-phone number, which I give students to use in the case of an emergency. Well, this was an emergency. As I gradually roused myself from a sound sleep, I heard him talking, clearly upset.

"This is Marcus in your LPN program, and I need help," he said.

"What's wrong?" I said in a voice intended to calm him down.

But he just went on, "Oh, my God. What am I going to do? What am I going to do?"

Finally, after I said, "What do you mean?" he calmed down enough to tell me.

"I went outside to drive my kids to day care so I could get to school in time. But all four of my tires were slashed."

He was very upset, and after I calmed him down again, he explained what made the situation even worse.

"I have a final exam today, and I have to pass it to stay in the program. And I don't have any more allowed days to take off at work because I used them up when my kids were sick. So I could lose my job too. My employer is paying my tuition, so I have to pass this class."

There was a simple solution—he just needed a ride, since he didn't have the money to pay for a cab.

I told him to get ready. "I'll have a cab pick you and the kids up, take them to day care, and then bring you to the school," I said. "I'll pay for it and also loan you the money to get your tires replaced."

"Thank you, thank you," he said, relieved he could see a way out of his problem.

Later that morning, Marcus came to school in a cab and passed the final exam with a high grade, and then he graduated a few months later. Soon afterward, he got his first job as an LPN. He made a down payment and took out a loan to buy a new home for himself and the kids.

About seven years later, in 2012, he came to see me and proudly told me that he was now a registered nurse working at a hospital and making more than $70,000 a year. It was quite a change from the days when he was just getting by on welfare, and all he needed was a ride to class.

THE SLEEPY STUDENT

Sometimes the pace of school and balancing it with a personal life can be tiring. That's what happened to one student I'll call Maggie who had to sleep things off, which led to a police report regarding a missing student. It all started about two weeks before a graduation ceremony, when we had an evening class that ended at 10:30 p.m. At the time, our campus was housed in several buildings: a model home, a building with a classroom on one side and skills laboratory on the other, and third, smaller building that I had just rented to be used for a library and some small offices.

The class took a break for dinner. After the students returned from getting food at a nearby grocery store, they returned to the small student lounge in the building with the classrooms. As the other students relaxed and chatted over dinner, Maggie, who'd been working an 11:00 p.m. to 7:00 a.m. shift, walked over to the back building, which was open, because she needed to take a quick nap. She settled down to rest in one of the small rooms, which was set up as a patient's hospital room. Meanwhile, the class returned for the rest of the lecture, with no one noticing that she hadn't returned to class. When the class let out at 10:30 p.m., no one noticed that her car was still in the driveway either.

That was because she was sound asleep in the back building. After class, Maggie's husband grew very concerned that she hadn't returned home, so he called the instructor to ask about his missing wife.

The instructor called me at 12:30 a.m. in a panic. "One of our students didn't come home tonight," she blurted out. "Maggie's husband just called me, and her car is still in the school parking lot."

I immediately jumped into my car and drove to the school, where a police car was parked in the driveway, just behind Maggie's car. The officers began to search the buildings, shining a light through each window. I went around with my keys, opening locked doors for them so they could check each classroom and office one by one.

Finally, I took the police to the back building, which was where they found Maggie asleep on a hospital bed in one of the small offices. An officer shined his light on her, but she continued to sleep soundly—at least they could hear her breathing. The officer went over and called her name.

At once Maggie awoke, muttering, "What's wrong?"

We were all just happy she was OK. The police escorted her back to her car, and soon she was on her way back to her husband. Case closed.

After that, everyone called Maggie "Sleepy," though she successfully graduated without falling asleep and is now a registered nurse with a master's degree.

MY FATHER'S CAREGIVERS

Over the years, I've become a mentor to our students, and they've mentored me as well. I love what I've accomplished, and every day I smile and thank God for the vision and the pure drive not to give up, even when it might have been easier to do so. In the past, when I've talked about goals and being a visionary, I never imagined it would personally come around full circle.

This past year has been very emotional for me. My aunt died of brain cancer, and then, a few months later, my dad was diagnosed with stage-four bladder cancer—the big *C* word, the one no one wants to talk about. His time was quick. Within months of his diagnosis, he was gone. When I think about my blessings, one thing that comes to mind is that my father was amazing and kind and so much like my youngest son, because he never met a stranger and always seemed to find the best in others. Right before he died in January 2011, he was admitted into a nursing facility and then a hospital, and to my surprise, two of our former nursing students were taking care of him in his final days. When I walked into the facility, they immediately ran toward me, threw their arms around my neck, and hugged me for the longest time.

I felt a great calm knowing that when these young ladies had enrolled in our nursing program, they had no previous experience in health care, and neither of them could even take a blood pressure. But now they were taking care of one of the most important men in my life, my father. One was a beautiful young lady with a big smile and a heart to match; she was the class social butterfly. The other was always shy and quiet. They were always together.

As I walked into the unit where my father was being cared for, they proceeded to tell me how he was doing. In one breath they rattled off all the medical terminology they had learned at school; his blood pressure was 220 over 170, the doctor had increased his pain medication, blood had been drawn, and the lab values had come back with several abnormalities. They also described the disease process and my father's poor nutritional status. Listening to them, I was reminded that God had a purpose for me in enabling me to survive that horrible day in August 2002. Looking back today, I know I've always been outcome-driven, and the student nurses caring for my father were the greatest outcome that I never could have seen coming: having a loved one in the final days of his life being taken care of by young ladies who are now nurses because of my vision.

After explaining my father's condition, they went into his room, introduced themselves to him, and reminded him that they remembered he had come into the class so they could practice taking blood pressure on him. He smiled and replied, "Did you learn how yet?"

My students' care for him didn't stop there. He was eventually admitted to a hospice. The nurse who came to my father's home to make her initial visit was another of our graduates. She followed his care as a professional with compassion and skill, just as I knew she would. She was a part of our family until the very end.

KISSING A PIG
Sometimes our students have fun during or after school by creating special events, such as the time they decided that the person who received the most charitable donations in his or her name had to do what the class chose as a surprise.

The students had agreed to donate several hundred dollars to a local charity. Of course, since the money would go to a good cause, I agreed to join them in this endeavor, but I wasn't informed that if I raised the most money, I'd have to kiss a pig—and that's exactly what happened. The students got a pig from a nearby farm, and while a reporter from the local news watched, I stood on the front lawn as a student walked the large pig on a harness to us. Though the students had told me I'd be kissing a cute potbellied pig, my first reaction was that this was a monster, big enough to feed patrons at a barbecue restaurant for a week.

As I kneeled to give the pig a quick peck on the cheek, it turned to me with snot and slobber on its face, and I got snot all over my cheek! The photo of the pig and me ended up in the newspaper, though fortunately it was on the back page.

I was truly embarrassed, but the money went to a good cause, so I'd willingly do it again. I also felt this bit of making good fun of the administration helped create a warmer feeling between the students and me. I wasn't just some distant campus president who disconnected herself from the student body by locking myself in an office. Instead, my experience of kissing the pig created a closer bond between the students and me, which helped increase school spirit and built stronger camaraderie among all of us.

ONE SIMPLE ACT OF KINDNESS, AND NOW HE'S IN MEDICAL SCHOOL

As the campus president, I found it inspiring when I was able to help students overcome the obstacles standing in the way of achieving their dreams. For example, one day in fall 2013, a very nice local physician called to tell me he wanted to help his son get into medical school. But so far several local schools had turned him down.

The man went on to explain that his son was a senior in high school and needed to get some certifications to add to his medical-school application. He went on to explain that this young man's mother, grandfather, and father all were physicians. They were much respected in our community, and I was honored that he had called me.

I agreed to meet with his son, and a few days later, he came to talk with me. My first impression was that I might not be able to help in any way, but I was immediately impressed with his determination. He knew exactly what he wanted to do with his life, and he had a clear plan regarding how he would accomplish his goals. He explained that he had completed dual enrollments while still in high school, and he had earned more credits than most students achieve in two years of college—yet he hadn't even graduated from high school.

As he continued talking about his plans and what he hoped to do, I felt he would make an amazing doctor someday if he were given the chance. So I felt compelled to help his application stand out.

But how could I help his application stand out in the very competitive struggle to get into medical school? "As a college president, I'll give you a recommendation letter," I told him.

Then I asked one of the faculty members to come into my office, and I told her, "I'd like you to teach him phlebotomy, EKG, and CPR, whatever he needs to get additional certifications to include in his application." I also said, "Teach him around his school schedule, even on weekends; do whatever you have to." And she did.

The young man attended every class and was diligent in getting every certification possible, and condensing several months of classwork into a few short weeks. The instructor I had asked to help him had to postpone her other classes so she could devote every day to assisting him.

A few months later, when he filed his application, which included these added certifications from our college, to a top medical school with more than eighty applicants competing for twenty-four slots, he was accepted.

If his father hadn't called to ask for my help, would he still have been accepted? I'm not sure, but I do know I've never met a young man so determined to walk in his family's footsteps and so dedicated to the profession of medicine at such a young age. I'm very confident he'll have a successful career as a doctor. Although he has a few years until graduation, this young man has inspired me tremendously.

This experience reminded me that I'd been put in this place to change one person's life at a time, and as I did so, this young man changed mine by helping me realize I was fulfilling my purpose in building the college. If I were to ever wake up in a hospital as a patient, I wouldn't mind seeing him as my doctor.

THE COMEDIAN IN THE CLASS

Another former student I remember fondly worked part-time as a comedian, and he brought his comic skills into the classroom. He had a way of making everyone laugh, much like Robin Williams did in playing Patch Adams, the doctor who helped cheer up his pediatric patients who were dying of cancer by putting on a clown nose and telling jokes.

Well, that was what this former student, Rick, did by injecting humor into what might normally be a very dry lecture about anatomy, treatment options, rectal exams, placentas, or any other number of topics.

One day he must have woken up and thought, *I'm going to tell everyone how to give birth, from a man's perspective.* He walked into the classroom just as the instructor was starting her lecture about female anatomy. When Rick spoke about the vagina, he immediately described how a baby must feel going through the birth canal, floating in fluid and then rushing out as if he or she were white-water rafting. Rick went into such detail that soon the whole class was laughing. Their laughter became so loud and infectious that another class began listening to his stand-up comedy routine about the female reproductive system, which was displayed on a very pregnant maternal mannequin that delivered a baby's placenta and afterbirth. But because of all the jokes, the instructor never finished, and the baby was never delivered that day. Rather, Rick delivered a series of jokes that had the students in his class in an uproar, along with the instructor and students in several other classes.

But more than just telling jokes, Rick was a visionary. One day, soon after I'd completed the development of a program, we were talking in my office. He told me, "I really believe in your vision for the school." He continued boldly, telling me with a straight face exactly what he thought at that moment, when others might keep their thoughts to themselves. "You have a wonderful vision," he said, "but remember that a vision without a detailed plan is only a hallucination."

I assured him I would keep his thoughts in mind, and I did. His bold, honest comment reminded me that I should always have a plan in place for everything I do. I can't just have a dream; I have to work out the exact steps to make my vision happen.

That's what Rick did as well. After graduating, he became a caring nurse, using his humor to help cheer up his patients, and in the manner of Patch Adams, he's currently working in home health.

A BABY IN THE BATHROOM

Another incident I'll never forget is when a student named Jena's water broke in the bathroom during exam week. A number of students were gathered in the break room just prior to taking their final exams. Although Jena was in the last trimester of her pregnancy, we weren't prepared for her to deliver that day.

As Jena sat in the break room, her fellow students could tell she was grimacing in pain, though she made no complaints. She just was experiencing cramps and was unable to sit still.

Several students asked her, "Are you all right?"

Then one of them went and retrieved their instructor, who asked her, "Do you need to leave?"

Jena shook her head and said, "I'm OK."

The instructor told everyone it was time to start the final exam in medical-surgical nursing. As everyone filed into the classroom, Jena decided to go to the ladies' room one last time, since she'd been complaining that she'd had to urinate every few minutes all morning.

That was when she started having stronger and stronger contractions. She calmly walked into the bathroom, and a few minutes later, her water broke all over the floor. Another student walked in, saw her standing in a puddle of water, and went to get the instructor.

When the instructor arrived, she told Jena, "You need to get to the hospital right away."

The reply was shocking. The student said, "I've worked too hard for my grades. The baby will have to wait. I'm not leaving until I take my final exam."

Jena calmly walked back to class, sat down, and completed her exam. Afterward, another student drove her to the hospital, where she gave birth to a beautiful baby girl.

The birth became a common topic of conversation and gave rise to the phrase, "Pass an exam and have a baby—all in a day's work at our college."

Fortunately, Jena passed the exam with flying colors. She eventually became a registered nurse, working at a local hospital and making a six-figure salary as a single mother.

HER BOYFRIEND TOLD HER TO QUIT

Another student I remember fondly, Chantal, is a woman who was struggling in school. She came into my office crying, saying, "I'm ready to give up."

"Why? What's going on?" I asked.

She described what was making it so hard for her. "I have two kids at home, and I have to work full-time to go to school. And my boyfriend wants me to quit."

Then she cried some more, and I sensed she didn't want to quit but was having an extremely hard time juggling all her responsibilities.

"Are you out of your mind?" I shot back at her. "You have so many opportunities ahead of you. You'd be making a terrible mistake if you walked away from this school after all your hard work."

As Chantal muffled her tears, I went on.

"Look, first you have to take your boyfriend out of the equation, and don't let his opinion guide you. He might just be a temporary thing."

She looked at me as if I were crazy. "But I love him," she insisted.

I laughed at that and explained what she needed to do. "What's most important is that your children depend on you. You always can get another boyfriend. So stand on your own two feet and stop searching for someone to hold you up."

Chantal still wasn't sure, giving me excuses as to why she needed her boyfriend in her life. So I called her mother and told her that her daughter was about to drop out of college because of a new boyfriend she had met online. That was all her mother needed to know, and within thirty minutes, she was at the school in my office with her daughter.

We all talked. As the student cried some more, her mother reassured her that she should stay in school and think of her future, not her boyfriend, whom she'd only recently met.

"Think of your future and your kids," her mother yelled as I sat back and listened.

Then I told her, "Now get back to class."

She agreed to stay in school, and within three months, she graduated and became a nurse. In the spring of the following year, she came to see me at the college and told me how much she appreciated my standing up for her and not letting her quit.

"No one has ever stood up for me except my mother and you," she said.

Then she told me she was going to purchase her first house, and her boyfriend had left her within two months of our meeting.

As I watched her sitting before me, I swelled with pride thinking about her accomplishments and how I'd been instrumental in keeping her on course. In fact, I'd treated her as if she were my own child, and I was thrilled that she was now a registered nurse and enjoying an amazing career.

ALL SHE NEEDED WAS A CHANCE

I wasn't sure whether a young mother who was a prospective student could make it, so I gave her a challenge. In this case, Elena was working as a nursing assistant at a local nursing home. She never had finished high school and was working to support her children, though she was barely getting by at twelve dollars an hour. The administrator of the facility where she worked referred her to me to help her become a nurse, because she was an excellent nursing assistant.

When Elena initially walked into my office to talk with me, I was skeptical that she would be able to accomplish everything in the timeline necessary. After we talked, however, I was convinced she wouldn't give up, so I wanted to give her a chance.

"I'll let you into the program," I told her, "but you have to sign a letter of intent that promises me you'll get your GED at least one month before you graduate from nursing school. Then you can complete the program."

"Yes, I will," she assured me. "And thank you for giving me this chance."

After that, Elena not only took my challenge but also exceeded my expectations. Her schedule was arduous between working full-time, going to school full-time, taking GED courses, and raising her children alone. She impressed me by maintaining good grades, and within a month of her scheduled graduation date, she walked into my office and handed me her GED.

I hugged her and said, "I'm proud of you." My eyes welled up. "Congratulations. You did it, and that shows you can do whatever else you want if you set your mind to it."

That experience made me realize I needed to look outside the box and try my best to make a difference in someone else's life.

Several months later, Elena took her state boards and became a licensed practical nurse. Within two years she bought her first new car and house as a single mother. Then she met a wonderful man and got married.

Elena has proven to herself and everyone around her that she isn't a quitter. She reminded me of the challenges I had to face, and I'm grateful she came to me asking for a chance. She could easily have given up after having been previously denied access to an education by a local community college. Instead, all she needed was someone to believe in her and give her a plan. The rest was on her, and her determination was overpowering. I'll never forget this beautiful young lady who impacted my life as much as I impacted hers. She has also become a lifelong friend.

This experience is further proof that people are placed in our paths for a reason.

CONCLUDING THOUGHT

In reflecting on these stories, I feel that the life-changing events in the lives of my student graduates and the great number of patients they take care of every day are in some small way a testament to God's purpose for me. These many success stories have helped show me I've been on the right path in working toward fulfilling God's purpose.

CHAPTER 6
A NEW BEGINNING

As I sit and write this last chapter, I've come to realize that I've accomplished all my professional dreams and goals in thirteen short years.

Although these years haven't been the easiest, they've been momentous because I've learned many things from the friends around me. My best friend, Donna, taught me to remember that when things get bad, just breathe in and breathe out, and Dave taught me how to be a true friend with no expectations of anything in return. Greg and Denise taught me to always put God first in everything I do.

Learning from others has made me think about what I've learned about myself. I started a college from nothing but an idea that came from one tragic event.

Just recently, I've been able to fulfill a lifelong dream of spending several months traveling through Europe, meeting many people along the way and learning about their cultures. Taking this time off allowed me to see a clearer picture of the impact I've had on thousands of nursing and therapy graduates, as well as the many lives that each one has touched because of his or her education. This in itself continues to keep me humble while inspiring me to seek greater opportunities.

After the accident I became a different person—we all change over time. As we get older, hopefully we all become a little more mature. Personally, I've developed into much more of a linear thinker. I've also set a very high bar for my accomplishments, although sometimes I selectively choose not to see the day-to-day minutiae that surround my vision. If I did, I'm sure it would scare the heck out of me, which might make me not want to continue.

I've thrived on my obsession of bringing my dreams to fruition and building a licensed, accredited college. My husband still keeps asking me, "When is enough?" I just know that I'm unable to answer this question. As the college grew, so did the passion inside me to provide an education to those who otherwise wouldn't be able to attend a community college or university. It also fed my need to strive for perfection and work harder to achieve it. I continue to surround myself with wonderful people and employees, all of whom have walked alongside me in my journey, believing in me even when I didn't believe in myself, including my sons. I knew in my heart that if I failed at my attempts, these people would still love me for trying. They were my true inspiration.

Deciding what I was destined to accomplish with my life as an adult was somewhat complex. In fact, it took a life-changing event to make me realize that life has no boundaries except the ones we place on ourselves. I remember a conversation with my youngest son while he was in high school, just a few months from graduation. I asked him a silly question, and I deserved the answer he gave me. I asked, "What goals do you have after you graduate high school?"

His response was simple: "My goal is to have a goal." After I stood there, staring at him as he seriously considered how he would respond, it took every ounce of energy I had not to fall on the floor laughing in front of the guidance counselor at his school. This was his simple solution to the adult world of responsibilities and careers. Yes, he was only seventeen, but as a parent,

I thought he should have the next thirty years planned out—but then again, I didn't when I was his age. My career choices happened by accident—literally.

I love to hear people talk about their dreams and why they're important to them. Mostly they just need someone to listen and hear that someone believes in them. When you have a dream or plan for your future, and you think about each step it will take to accomplish your dream, if the idea doesn't scare you, you probably haven't thought it through. The problem is that when people want to accomplish something, they rarely follow through because they lack the drive or they're afraid of failure. But failure can come from many things, such as making a decision you know is wrong or not asking for advice. There are many resources available, and it takes courage to ask for help. Few people realize that they fail for lack of trying.

As I mentioned earlier in this book, simple words of encouragement can mean the difference between success and failure. If people fail at something, it doesn't define who they are, unless they embrace failure as a way out. Pick yourself up, refocus, and try again. Like most people, I've faced many challenges in my life. I now realize it wasn't the challenge itself but how I dragged myself through the challenge that defined me. Don't be the person who blames everyone else for what happens. Suck it up, take responsibility, pick yourself up, and try again—or move on with your life and don't dwell on what-ifs.

Over the years, I've spoken with hundreds of students who for one reason or another lacked the motivation to think about their future. When people want something badly enough, they can feel it, live it, and taste it—and then it becomes real and tangible.

After the long, arduous process of my rehabilitation and the lingering effects of my injuries, which will continue until my last breath, this chapter in the book of my life is closing, and new chapters are beginning, with so much more enthusiasm on my part to take on different challenges. I met and married a wonderful man who has an extensive background in physical therapy. He not only understands my physical limitations but also helps me move through the bad days. His ability to walk beside me, guiding each step even when my feet are numb, shows me that God had a purpose for his being in the profession he chose.

I've thought long and hard about where my path will lead next. I know the journey is going to be fun, but the excitement will come when I've developed my new purpose—the one that can touch many more lives than the college has and that will allow me to motivate others to be the very best they can be. I believe that will happen through my lectures, my consulting, and my written words. In this next chapter in my life, I'm destined for a much bigger purpose. I can only hope to affect many more lives and that my legacy in doing so will live on exponentially.

CONCLUDING THOUGHT

Over the years, I've been blessed to have my family by my side through the good and bad times. At times it's been overwhelming to suffer in silence from my lingering emotional, mental, and physical injuries, but it's made me a stronger person—the woman I now know I was always meant to become.

I hope my book has in some way inspired you to believe in yourself, trust in your abilities, never stop learning, give as much as you receive, and change course when your path leads you to a mud puddle.

DISCUSSION POINTS

I've included several questions below as topics of discussion. Please feel free to contact me at my website, www.dlynne.com.

1. Do you believe a life-and-death experience can change a person's perspective on living? If so, how?
2. What are your thoughts regarding a single mother with no college degree starting a college?
3. Was this book inspiring to you? If so, how?
4. While reading this book, did you laugh, cry, or smile? If so, which part did you enjoy the most?
5. Did this book inspire you to find your purpose or start a business?
6. Do you have any words of encouragement that you would like me to share with others?
7. Have you ever overcome a tragedy and used the experience to change the lives of others?
8. Have you ever survived a tragic accident?
9. Are you in the medical field? If so, which profession?
10. Would you be interested in having me speak at an event? If so, please contact me through the website above.

www.ingramcontent.com/pod-product-compliance
Lightning Source LLC
Chambersburg PA
CBHW062007040426
42447CB00010B/1950